Understanding
Working Memory

Understanding
Working Memory
2nd Edition

Tracy Packiam Alloway
Ross G. Alloway

Los Angeles | London | New Delhi
Singapore | Washington DC

Los Angeles | London | New Delhi
Singapore | Washington DC

SAGE Publications Ltd
1 Oliver's Yard
55 City Road
London EC1Y 1SP

SAGE Publications Inc.
2455 Teller Road
Thousand Oaks, California 91320

SAGE Publications India Pvt Ltd
B 1/I 1 Mohan Cooperative Industrial Area
Mathura Road
New Delhi 110 044

SAGE Publications Asia-Pacific Pte Ltd
3 Church Street
#10-04 Samsung Hub
Singapore 049483

Editor: Jude Bowen/Amy Jarrold
Associate editor: Miriam Davey
Production editor: Nicola Marshall
Copyeditor: Elaine Leek
Marketing manager: Lorna Patkai
Cover design: Wendy Scott
Typeset by: C&M Digitals (P) Ltd, Chennai, India
Printed in Great Britain by Henry Ling Limited, at
the Dorset Press, Dorchester, DT1 1HD

Library of Congress Control Number: 2014936742

British Library Cataloguing in Publication data

A catalogue record for this book is available from
the British Library

MIX
Paper from
responsible sources
FSC™ C013985
www.fsc.org

ISBN 978–1–4462–7420–0
ISBN 978–1–4462–7421–7 (pbk)

At SAGE we take sustainability seriously. Most of our products are printed in the UK using FSC papers and boards.
When we print overseas we ensure sustainable papers are used as measured by the Egmont grading system.
We undertake an annual audit to monitor our sustainability.

We dedicate this book to our boys, who remind us daily of the delight that learning and discovery bring.

CONTENTS

LIST OF FIGURES

ABOUT THE AUTHORS

Tracy Packiam Alloway, PhD, is a professor of psychology at the University of North Florida. Formerly, she was the director of the Centre for Memory and Learning in the Lifespan (at the University of Stirling) in the UK. She is an expert on working memory and education, and has published more than 75 journal articles and books on this topic. She developed the internationally recognized Automated Working Memory Assessment (Pearson Assessment, translated into 20 languages). She writes a blog for *Psychology Today* and the *Huffington Post*. She has also provided advice to Fortune 500 companies, such as Prudential, as well as the World Bank and BBC.
www.tracyalloway.com

Ross Alloway, PhD, CEO of Memosyne Ltd, brings working memory training to educators and parents. Ross developed *Jungle Memory*™, used by thousands of students in more than 20 countries. Together with Tracy Alloway, Ross edited an academic book on working memory (Psychology Press) and co-authored a popular science book (Simon & Schuster, translated into 17 languages). He has also published research with Tracy Alloway on working memory in a variety of contexts, from education to aging, from happiness to lying, from barefoot running to Facebook. Their research has been featured on the BBC, *ABC News*, the *Huffington Post*, *Salon*, the *Washington Post*, and *Newsweek*. He writes a blog for the *Huffington Post*.
www.docsalloway.com

Evan Copello was a student researcher in Dr. Tracy Alloway's lab at the University of North Florida. He collaborated with Tracy Alloway on multiple projects, including a cross-cultural project investigating standardized testing in college students, and nonverbal deception and working memory in children. He was the President of the International Honors Society in Psychology, Psi Chi (2013–2014).

Kim Phillips Grant has an undergraduate degree in Honors Psychology from Saint Mary's University in Halifax, Nova Scotia and a Specialist Graduate degree in School Psychology from the University of Kansas. She has been a practicing school psychologist in a large, suburban school district in northeastern Kansas for nine years. Putting her passion with working memory to work, she won a grant from her school district foundation to develop and coordinate a district wide program for screening, intervening, and assessing students for working memory difficulties.

ACKNOWLEDGEMENTS

We are grateful to the thousands of teachers and parents who have contacted us and taken us beyond the world of theory and data to see the classroom from your perspective. While we have changed the names in the case studies for the sake of anonymity, we are so glad that you have allowed us to pass along your story as part of this journey. Your struggles and successes have inspired and motivated us to keep searching for answers to find out what makes the difference for students.

Our road to discovering the importance of working memory in learning has been shared with so many people and we have been inspired by many colleagues in the trenches: school psychologists like Kim Grant and Misty Swanger, who are so passionate about supporting their students' working memory; and professionals like Denise Yates in NAGC Britain and Carol Brown at the Academic Success Center of Kentucky, who work tirelessly to communicate research with parents.

The team at SAGE Publications has been simply wonderful. Jude Bowen and Amy Jarrold at SAGE Publications have been a fantastic support and it has been a real joy to work with them. They have been supportive from the beginning of this project and their constant encouragement has been brilliant. We are truly lucky to have you both as such champions for this book! Many thanks to Nicola Marshall and Elaine Leek for their careful editorial comments, to Lorna Patkai for her suggestions for the videos that accompany this book, and to Miriam Davey for her assistance throughout.

We would like to give special thanks to Evan Copello, the lead researcher in Tracy's lab. He has crafted the wonderful case studies for Chapters 3 to 8 based on his involvement with several organizations that support learning disorders. His compassion for students with learning needs translates beyond the classroom and he has greatly enriched this book, from crafting the case studies to bouncing ideas around and proofreading multiple drafts. Margo Bristow and Miquela Elsworth have also shared their experiences from their research projects. Tracy's 5th grade class in an international school gave her the first experience of teaching and she loved it!

We have been fortunate to be part of many fruitful collaborations that demonstrate how evidence-based practice can change a student's life. Thank you to all the schools that have invited us to share this research with you. This book would not have been written if it weren't for your interest in working memory.

CHAPTER 1

OUR BRAIN'S POST-IT NOTE

This chapter looks at:

- WHAT is working memory?
- WHERE is working memory in the brain?
- WHY is working memory linked to learning?

My (Tracy's) journey began, on a crisp October day about 10 years ago.

I was surrounded by a sea of small and eager faces, the children all in neatly pressed uniforms. As part of a government-funded project, I was working with kindergarteners to understand what cognitive skills are important for academic success.

I met Andrew that day. That 6-year-old boy stood out from the rest. He loved being at school and made friends quickly. In the classroom, he was always excited about participating and would raise his hand to answer questions. Andrew enjoyed 'story time' best, when Mrs Smith would ask the children to present a short story. Andrew loved telling stories and would be so animated and use such creative examples that all the children enjoyed them as well.

As the school year progressed, I noticed that Andrew began to struggle with daily classroom activities. He would often forget simple instructions or get them mixed up. When all the other children were putting their books away and getting ready for the next activity, Andrew would be standing in the middle of room, looking around confused. When Mrs Smith asked him why he was standing there, he just shrugged his shoulders. She tried asking him to write down the instructions so he could remember what to do. But by the time he got back to his desk, he had forgotten what he was supposed to write down.

His biggest problem seemed to be in writing activities. He would often get confused and repeat his letters. Even spelling his name was a struggle, he would write it with two 'A's or miss out the 'W' at the end. Mrs Smith tried moving him closer to the board so he could follow along better. This didn't seem to work; he would still get confused.

Mrs Smith was at a loss. She always had to repeat instructions to Andrew but he never seemed to listen. It was as if her words went in one ear and out the other. On another occasion an assistant found him at his desk not working. When she asked him why he wasn't doing the assignment, he hung his head and said, 'I've forgotten. Sometimes I get mixed up and I am worried that teacher will get angry at me.'

His parents contacted me to see if I could help. They were concerned that Andrew might have a learning disability. When I tested Andrew on a range of psychological tests, I was surprised to find that he had an average IQ. Yet, by the end of the school year, he was at the bottom of the class.

Two years later, I went back to the school to conduct some follow-up testing on the children. Andrew seemed like such a different boy. He was placed in the lowest ability groups for language and math. He became frustrated more easily and would not even attempt some activities, especially if they involved writing. His grades were poor and he often handed in incomplete work. He only seemed happy on the playground.

Although I wasn't able to follow up on Andrew, I never forgot him. His predicament inspired me to deeply research how we can support thousands of students who, like Andrew, struggle in class through no fault of their own. This book is about a powerful cognitive skill called working memory that, when properly supported, can stop students like Andrew from remembering their school years as a frustrating experience.

A foundational classroom skill

It is hard to conceive of a classroom activity that does not involve working memory – our ability to work with information. In fact, it would be impossible for students to learn without working memory. From following instructions to reading a sentence, from sounding out an unfamiliar word to calculating a math problem, nearly everything a student does in the classroom requires working with information. Even when a student is asked to do something simple, like take out their science book and open it to page 289, they have to use their working memory. They have to work with a number of pieces of information, including looking for the book in the right place, such as recalling that it is in their desk and not in their backpack, identifying which book is in fact their science book, and finally guesstimating where among the thick stack of pages they are most likely to find the correct one. If they overestimate or underestimate, they have to use their working memory to adjust, and flip forwards or backwards until they finally find page 289.

Most children have a working memory that is strong enough to quickly find the book and open to the correct page, but some don't – approximately 10% in any classroom. A student who loses focus and often daydreams may fall in this 10%. A student who isn't living up to their potential may fall in this 10%. A student who may seem unmotivated may fall in this 10%. In the past, many of these students would have languished at the bottom of the class, because their problems seemed insurmountable and a standard remedy like extra tuition didn't solve them. But emerging evidence shows that many of these children can improve their performance by focusing on their working memory. Working memory is a foundational skill in the classroom and when properly supported it can often turn around a struggling student's prospects.

WHAT: What is working memory?

One way to think of working memory is as the brain's 'Post-it note'. We make mental scribbles of what we need to remember. In addition to remembering information, we also use working memory to process or manage that information, even in the face of distraction. In a busy classroom, with classmates talking, pencils dropping, and papers rustling, the student has to use their working memory to ignore the activity around them and focus on what they need to accomplish.

Working memory is critical for a variety of activities at school, from reading comprehension and math to copying from the board and navigating around school. In the classroom, we use **verbal working memory** to remember instructions, learn language, and complete reading comprehension tasks. **Visual–spatial working memory** is linked to math skills and remembering sequences of patterns, images, and locations. Below are specific examples of activities requiring working memory taken from real classrooms.

Classroom activities that involve verbal working memory

- Remembering and carrying out lengthy instructions. Here is an example from a classroom of 6-year-olds: *Put your sheets on the green table, put the arrow cards in the packet, put your pencil away, and come and sit on the carpet.* Students with poor working memory are usually the first ones to sit down on the carpet – because they carried out only the first part of the instruction but forgot the rest!
- Remembering and writing down text, including words, sentences, and paragraphs.
- Remembering word lists that sound similar (example: *mat, man, map, mad*).
- Remembering sentences with complicated grammatical structure, such as *To save the princess, the knight fought the dragon*, which is harder to understand than *The knight fought the dragon **to save the princess.***

Classroom activities that involve visual–spatial working memory

- Solving a mental math problem.
- Keeping track of their place when writing a sentence from the board. The student with poor working memory will often repeat or skip letters.
- Using pictures or images to retell a story. The student with poor working memory may get confused about the order of events in the story or even leave out key events.
- Identifying missing numbers in a sequence: *0, 1, 2, __, 4, 5, __.*

Working memory versus short-term memory

Working memory is distinct from short-term memory, which lets you remember information for a brief time, usually a few seconds. Students use short-term memory when they look at something on the board, like 42 + 18, and remember it long enough to write it down. But they use their working memory to solve the problem, for example, by adding 40 to 10, holding 50 in mind, next adding 2 to 8, and adding both answers to get 60. Think of working memory as **'work'**-ing with information to remember.

Working memory versus long-term memory

Working memory is also distinct from long-term memory. For a student, long-term memory includes the library of knowledge they have accumulated in the course of their academic career. This may be math facts ($6 \times 4 = 24$), spelling rules ('i' before 'e' except after 'c'), scientific and historical knowledge, or the different sounds that phonemes make. Working memory is like a librarian who pulls the appropriate knowledge out of their library when it is needed. For example, if you ask a student to name the first president of the United States, it is their working memory that searches through their long-term memory and finds 'George Washington'.

Try It: Verbal working memory

Read these sentences and decide if they are true or false:

1. Bananas live in water: true or false?
2. Flowers smell nice: true or false?
3. Dogs have four legs: true or false?

Now, without looking at those sentences, can you remember the last word in each sentence in the correct order? If you were able to remember them, congratulate yourself. Your working memory is like that of an average 7-year-old. This test is an example of the Listening Recall test from the Automated Working Memory Assessment. It measures verbal (auditory) working memory.

In this book, **verbal working memory** is synonymous with **auditory working memory**. In tests like this, the sentences are presented verbally and the student repeats the information out loud. In Chapter 2, we look at standardized tests to identify working memory deficits.

WHERE it is: Working memory and the brain

Brain imaging has confirmed that when we perform working memory tests, like the one in the Try It box, there is activity in the prefrontal cortex (PFC). The PFC also works with other areas of the brain when we use working memory. For example, when we engage in visual–spatial activities like navigating to a new restaurant, the hippocampus (the home of spatial information) is activated as our working memory draws on it to determine where we currently are, and where we need to go. When we engage in verbal information, like answering questions in a job interview, our working memory draws on 'language centers' such as Broca's area, in order to craft an appropriate response.

Working memory growth

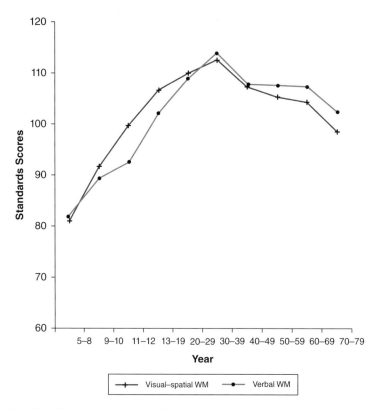

Figure 1.1   Working memory growth

Working memory growth is closely aligned with the development of the prefrontal cortex. We conducted a study with hundreds of participants from 5 to 80 years old to find out more about how working memory grows at each age (Figure 1.1). The most dramatic growth is during childhood – working memory increases more in the first 10 years than it does over the lifespan. There is also a steady increase in working memory capacity up to our thirties. At this point, working memory reaches a peak and plateaus. The average 25-year-old can successfully remember about five or six items. As we get older, working memory capacity declines to around three to four items.

The amount of information that working memory can process at each age has important implications for the classroom. A teacher attending a seminar Tracy gave in Seattle commented that she now understood why her class found it difficult to complete what she asked them to do. Here is an example of instructions she had given to her class: *Put your notebooks on the table, put colored pencils back in the drawer, get your lunchbox, and make a line by the door.* Instead of forming neat lines by the classroom door after putting away their books, they would wander around the class. 'I know why now: I would always give them four things to do at a time and it was too much for their working memory', she said after learning about the average space we have in our working memory at each age. Here is a quick guide for tailoring classroom instructions for working memory capacity at different ages:

- 5–6 years: 2 instructions
- 7–9 years: 3 instructions
- 10–12 years: 4 instructions
- 13–15 years: 5 instructions
- 16–29 years: 6 instructions

Up until our thirties, working memory is constantly increasing in size. It is getting bigger, which means we can process more information on our mental Post-it note. But some people's working memory grows faster than others. Think of a 7-year-old with a high working memory. Imagine a 10-year-old in a class of 7-year-olds. They are bored with what the teacher is saying and they finish assignments before anyone else. They may even act out because they have nothing else to do. This is exactly what it is like for a student with a higher working memory than his or her peers. About 10% of your class will fall in this group.

Let's look at the other end of the scale – the student with a poor working memory. Now imagine a 4-year-old in that class of 7-year-olds. They would be frustrated like the 10-year-old, but for the opposite reason: lessons are too hard to understand so they give up trying. The teacher is talking too fast for them to keep up; they can't spell all the words he or she is saying; they are struggling with adding up the numbers in the math problems; and they can't read the required text. Students with poor working memory often struggle in classroom activities because they are unable to hold in mind all the necessary information to complete the activity. As a result, they will disengage from learning.

WHY working memory predicts grades

Working memory is so important for learning that by knowing a student's working memory we can predict their grades throughout their academic career. As part of a large government-funded study (Alloway et al., 2006), hundreds of kindergarteners (5- to 6-year-olds) were tracked over a 6-year period and it was found that the children with high working memory did well in reading, writing, and math; while those with low working memory struggled in these tasks. Six years later, these students were tested again and their working memory ability at 5 years old was shown to determine how well they performed in standardized assessments of reading and math (Alloway and Alloway, 2010).

Think about your classroom. Some students perform better than others. Why is it so easy for the girl sitting in the front, but so hard for the student to her right? They all sit through the same lesson, yet have very different results. To answer this question, a group of 8- to 11-year-olds with learning disabilities were tracked over a 2-year period (Alloway, 2009). Even though they were receiving extra educational support, like tutoring and special classes, they were still performing at the bottom of the class. Their learning outcomes had not improved and they were still struggling. Students also became more frustrated and this was manifested in behavior problems. Why didn't they show any improvement? A closer look at their working memory scores revealed that all of them had low working memory scores and their working memory deficits meant that they could not fully absorb the information. It was like entering a bike race with flat tires: without any support for their working memory, they weren't able to make much progress in their learning.

Working memory and IQ

IQ is not nearly as reliable as working memory in predicting grades. This finding is important as it suggests that IQ, still viewed as a key predictor of academic success, is not a useful benchmark of success. An individual can have an average IQ score but perform poorly in learning, as we saw with Andrew at the beginning of this chapter. This is because IQ tests measure knowledge that students have already learned. If students do well on one of these tests, it is because they know the information they are tested on.

A commonly used measure of IQ is a vocabulary test. If they know the definition of a word like *bicycle* or *police*, then they will likely get a high IQ score. However, if they don't know the definitions of these words or perhaps don't articulate them well, this will be reflected in a low IQ score. In this way, IQ tests are very different from working memory tests because they measure how much students know and how well they can articulate this knowledge.

IQ test scores are strongly driven by a child's background and experiences. One research project involved two different schools: one was in an urban, developed area, while the other was in an underprivileged neighborhood (Alloway et al., 2014). As part of the project, students' IQ skills were tested using a vocabulary test. One of the vocabulary words – *police* – drew very different responses. Students from the urban school provided definitions relating to safety or uniforms, which corresponded to the examples in the manual. However, those from the underprivileged neighborhood responded with statements like *I don't like police* or *They are bad because they took my dad away*. Although both responses were drawn directly from the children's experiences, only one type of answer matched the IQ manual's definitions.

Working memory is a better predictor of success than IQ because it measures a student's **potential to learn.** A common working memory test is to remember a sequence of numbers in the reverse order that it was presented to you. If students struggle in this test, it is not because they don't know how to count, or don't understand number magnitude. It doesn't even matter whether they can recognize the numbers. If they struggle in this working memory test, it is often because their mental 'Post-it note' isn't big enough to remember three or four numbers. Working memory is a better predictor of success than IQ from kindergarten to college because it measures students' ability to learn, rather than what they have learned.

Science Flash: Working memory and impulse control

Working memory is also linked to a very important skill: impulse control. In a series of well-publicized studies from the 1960s, Stanford psychologist Walter Mischel offered more than 600 children between the ages of 4 and 6 a marshmallow. Then he told them that he was going to leave the room, and if they could wait until he returned, they would get a second marshmallow. If they could not wait, they could ring a little bell that he left on the table, and he would return and let them eat the one marshmallow. Some of the children immediately popped the marshmallow into their mouths while others resisted temptation and held out for the greater reward of two marshmallows. Resisting the temptation to eat the marshmallow involves working memory as the children had to come up with a plan to distract themselves from the thought of eating the marshmallow.

(Continued)

(Continued)

Mischel tracked these children over the years and found that their ability to control their impulses played an important role later in life. For example, in a 1990 follow-up study, children who had better impulse control and waited for that second marshmallow had higher scores in a standardized achievement test (SAT). He also tested them as adults and put them in a brain scanner while they were performing cognitive tasks involving impulse control. He found that the adults who had resisted the marshmallow temptation as children were more likely to show activation in their prefrontal cortex, the home of working memory, while they were performing a similar impulse control as adults. However, the adults who were not able to resist the marshmallow temptation as children did not show activation in the prefrontal cortex. Working memory is an important cognitive skill that we use to control our impulses and make good decisions, which can help us achieve our long-term goals.

Working memory deficits

Ben walks through the door, nervous and dreading the moment when his mother is going to ask the question he knows is coming: 'Can I see your report card?' He takes it out of his backpack with sweaty hands. His mother reads the results of a semester's worth of work, and sighs, 'We'll try harder next time'. Unfortunately, trying harder isn't going to make a difference. Many students like Ben try hard every day and still struggle.

Students like Ben haven't been diagnosed with a learning disorder, though they have lower grades. Often when a student is performing poorly, teachers and psychologists look for evidence of a particular problem, like ADHD or dyslexia. When the evidence isn't found, the student is often misunderstood as 'lazy' and unwilling to put in the effort necessary for success. It is important to recognize that many of these students have a poor working memory, and no amount of effort is going to improve their grades if their working memory isn't supported.

Working memory affects all areas of learning, from language to math, from history to art. No matter how hard Ben tries, he will not 'catch up' with his peers. If a child has low grades in kindergarten as a result of their working memory, they will almost certainly have poor grades all the way through high school. One study (Alloway, 2009) found that teenagers who had been diagnosed with working memory deficits two years previously were still performing very poorly in school.

As students get older, the learning gap widens and they will continue to struggle throughout their academic career. A struggling 6-year-old with working memory deficits is unlikely to catch up with peers without intervention . A government-funded study comparing 6- and 11-year-olds with working memory deficits found that the effect of poor working memory is cumulative, resulting in greater decrements in learning as a student gets older (Alloway et al., 2009).

This difference in performance can be explained in part by the classroom environment of the two age groups. Younger children are more likely to have additional adult support and memory aids made available for them in the classroom. However, as they get older, they are typically expected to be more independent in their learning and may be left to develop their own strategies. Among older students, teachers are also more likely to use longer and more complex sentences, which require the students to rely on their working memory. Their poor working memory means that they struggle to acquire key learning skills and concepts. Without these building blocks in place, they are unable to keep up with their peers. As they get older, the combination of the increasing difficulty of their class work and an insufficient learning foundation results in them lagging behind their peers.

This is why early diagnosis and support is so crucial. It is not unusual to encounter parents of college-age students who with tears in their eyes say how they wished they had known about working memory when their child was younger, how much it could have helped them, and how much they struggle just to pass a test now they are in college. The good news is that we can change their grades by changing their working memory.

Working memory and learning disabilities

Some students have poor working memory and a learning disability as well. In fact, if a student has a learning disability, they also have a poor working memory. Thus students with learning disabilities have a **double deficit**: they have a 'core problem' and a working memory deficit. Each of the learning disabilities included in this book has a very different 'core problem'. For example, students with dyslexia are characterized by reading difficulties; those with dyscalculia struggle with math; students with developmental coordination disorder (DCD) have motor impairments, those with ADHD find it hard to inhibit and control their behavior, individuals with autistic spectrum disorder have a restricted range of language and social skills; and those with an anxiety disorder can experience a working memory overload due to worrisome thoughts.

Given their distinctive profile, what do these groups have in common? All of them have a weakness in working memory (Figure 1.2). That is not to say that poor working memory causes the core deficit in their respective disorder. However, it coexists as a separate problem and ultimately leads to learning difficulties. For example, a deficit in working memory does not cause motor problems in the student with DCD, but their weak working memory leads to learning difficulties (Chapter 5). Throughout this book, we will learn that each group has a specific area of working memory strength and weakness, and when we know what this is, we can provide targeted support to maximize learning.

Each disorder included in this book – reading and math disabilities, DCD, ADHD, autistic spectrum disorder, and anxiety disorders – appears in some form in the *Diagnostic and Statistical Manual of Mental Disorders* (now in its fifth edition and known as *DSM-5,* APA, 2013). This volume, published by the American Psychiatric Association, is the

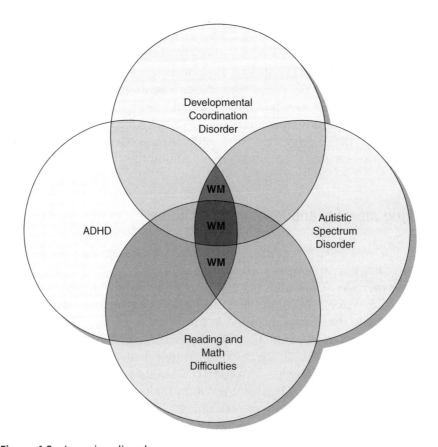

Figure 1.2   Learning disorders

leading reference manual for disorders, and the diagnostic criteria provide a valuable and trusted resource used by clinicians, researchers, and related professionals around the world. Inclusion in *DSM-5* goes some way in validating the existence of the disorder. As a result of being diagnosed with a disorder that appears in *DSM-5*, the student can be entitled to special education-needs provision. It is often the case that if a link can be demonstrated between the disorder and detrimental learning outcomes, then a case can be made for qualifying for support.

Overview of the book

Each of the following chapters includes a description of the learning difficulty (WHAT), followed by an inside look into the brain of a student with the disorder (WHERE), their unique working memory profile (WHY), and classroom strategies to support working memory (HOW). There are two types of strategies: **general working memory strategies** that can be applied to all students in your class, and **specific working memory strategies** for each learning difficulty. The final chapter (Chapter 9) provides the student with tools to empower them along their learning journey. The aim in supporting students with learning difficulties is not just to help them survive in the classroom, but to thrive as well. The strategies in the book can provide scaffolding and support that will unlock their working memory potential to boost learning. They are designed to be easily integrated within the classroom setting as a dimension of an inclusive curriculum and used in developing an individualized education program (IEP) for the student. The strategies recommended here can also complement existing programs that support a core deficit, such as a social skills program for a student with autistic spectrum disorder, or behavior modification for those with ADHD. Each chapter also includes:

- *Try It* box: Provides the reader with an opportunity to have a hands-on understanding of the material
- *Science Flash* box: Gives the reader a snapshot of current and interesting research related to each chapter
- *Current Debate* box: Discusses a controversial issue pertaining to the disorder

Working memory needs teachers like you. To have any impact, all the research published in hundreds of peer-reviewed articles, book chapters, and books over the past two decades needs teachers willing to take a chance, to look out for students with working memory problems, and to support their needs. Working memory is a foundational cognitive skill, but it needs you to make the difference.

Summary

1. Working memory is our ability to 'work' with information; think of it like your brain's *Post-it note*.
2. Working memory is a better predictor of academic success than IQ because it measures a student's **potential** to learn, not what they have already learned.
3. Working memory deficits are present in a range of learning disorders, from reading and math disabilities to developmental coordination disorder, ADHD, autistic spectrum disorder, and anxiety disorders.

References and further reading

Alloway, T.P. (2009) Working memory, but not IQ, predicts subsequent learning in children with learning difficulties. *European Journal of Psychological Assessment*, 25: 92–8.

Alloway, T.P. and Alloway, R.G. (2010) Investigating the predictive roles of working memory and IQ in academic attainment. *Journal of Experimental Child Psychology*, 106: 20–9.

Alloway, T.P., Gathercole, S.E., and Pickering, S.J. (2006) Verbal and visuospatial short-term and working memory in children: are they separable? *Child Development*, 77: 1698–716.

Alloway, T.P., Gathercole, S.E, Kirkwood, H.J., and Elliott, J.E. (2009) The cognitive and behavioral characteristics of children with low working memory. *Child Development, 80*: 606–21.

Alloway, T.P., Alloway, R.G., and Wootan, S. (2014) Home sweet home: Does where you live matter to working memory and other cognitive skills? *Journal of Experimental Child Psychology*, 124: 124–31.

APA (American Psychiatric Association) (2013) *Diagnostic and Statistical Manual of Mental Disorders: DSM-5*. Washington, DC: American Psychiatric Association.

Cowan, N. and Alloway, T.P. (2008) The development of working memory in childhood, in M. Courage and N. Cowan (eds), *Development of Memory in Infancy and Childhood*, 2nd edn. Hove: Psychology Press.

Gathercole, S.E. and Alloway, T.P. (2008) *Working Memory and Learning: A Practical Guide*. London: Sage.

Swanson, L. and Alloway, T.P. (2010) Working memory, learning, and academic achievement, in K. Harris, T. Urdan and S. Graham (eds), *APA Educational Psychology Handbook*, Vol. 1. Mahwah, NJ: Erlbaum.

CHAPTER 2

DIAGNOSING WORKING MEMORY

This chapter looks at:

- Standardized tests to screen for working memory deficits.
- Using classroom behavior to understand working memory difficulties.
- Standardized IQ tests that include working memory subtests.

Educators are growing increasingly aware that some of their students have working memory difficulties that can impact their learning (Alloway et al., 2012). In any given classroom 10–15% of students have working memory problems, though very few of them are identified (Alloway et al., 2009a). This is because most working memory tests require experience in psychometric testing and are part of standardized IQ tests that are labor intensive for the test administrator. Because a limited number of people have qualifications to administer such tests, only a relatively small number of students have been given the tests – far fewer than have working memory problems. The majority of students with working memory problems remain unidentified. Without knowing who these students are, we are not able to support them, and many of them will end up struggling throughout their academic career. But in the last decade, a powerful scientific tool called the Automated Working Memory Assessment (AWMA: Alloway, 2007a) has been made available to teachers and school psychologists who are interested in being proactive in their students' cognitive health by accurately measuring their students' working memory.

Automated Working Memory Assessment (AWMA)

The AWMA was designed in order to allow those who are unfamiliar with psychometric testing to administer the test, so that students who are in the greatest need of an accurate working memory diagnosis will no longer fall through the cracks. The features of the AWMA are discussed below.

Automated: The AWMA is an automated, computerized assessment. It is very easy to administer and requires little involvement on the part the administrator. The teacher or psychologist enters the student's details, such as their name and date of birth, and clicks on *Start* to begin. There are three versions:

- Screener (5–10 minutes)
- Short form (20 minutes)
- Long form (30 minutes)

When the student finishes, the AWMA automatically produces a detailed report of the student's working memory profile, including easy-to-interpret standard scores and percentiles. A benefit of the fully automated feature of the AWMA is reduced experimenter error, in both the administration and scoring of the working memory tests.

Working memory: Working memory in the classroom can be divided into two basic components – **verbal working memory** (words/language, numbers) and **visual–spatial working memory** (shapes, patterns, and number lines). It is very helpful for a teacher to know their students' visual and verbal working memory profiles, because they allow them to address individual students' strengths and weaknesses. For example, if you know that a student has poor verbal working memory, you can give them shorter instructions, which will allow them to keep on task with their classmates. If you know that a student struggles with visual–spatial working memory, you know that it will impact their math performance so you can develop their number sense so they can spend their working memory space on solving the problem.

Varied stimuli: The AWMA tests both verbal and visual–spatial working memory using a variety of stimuli. For example, tests of verbal working memory include both letters and numbers, and the visual–spatial working memory tests include dot locations and three-dimensional arrays of blocks. The AWMA uses more than one form of stimulus to make sure that test results accurately reflect their working memory, and provides a comprehensive assessment of working memory. This is particularly useful for students with learning difficulties as their core deficit may influence their working memory performance. For example, a student with math difficulties may perform worse on a number-based test. However, the inclusion of a verbal working memory using letters can reveal their working memory capacity independent of their weakness with numbers.

Pure measure: Some standardized working memory tests use sentences as their stimuli. But this may make the assessment inaccurate because research has established that we can remember almost twice as much information in sentence form than when it is a random string of words, letters, or numbers. For example, we can remember *The fox crawled through the grass and under the log* much better than if the same words were in random order: *under, the, through, fox, the, and, the, grass, log, crawled.* The semantic and grammatical cues in the sentence make it much easier to recall. Working memory tests that make use of sentences can artificially boost working memory performance, and the true nature of a working memory deficit may remain unidentified.

In contrast, the verbal working memory tests in the AWMA use random letters, words, and numbers, which provide no such cues to boost recall. Consequently, it is considered as a 'pure' measure of working memory capacity, and it can better determine the size of a student's working memory space.

Span procedure: The AWMA uses a span procedure for testing, which makes the test suitable for both children and adults. The number of items a person can remember and process progressively increases until the individual begins to struggle. The number of items they can correctly remember and process determines their working memory capacity, and the AWMA stops the testing process once the student has reached their limit.

Try It: Automated Working Memory Assessment (AWMA)

Verbal working memory

Ask a friend to say this letter: B. Now look at the letter in Figure 2.1. Was it the same letter as the one you just heard?

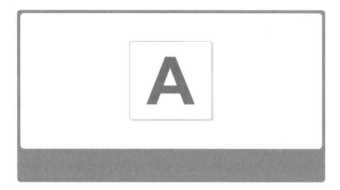

Figure 2.1 Verbal working memory

Now do you remember the letter you heard?

Visual–spatial working memory

Look at Figure 2.2. Is Mr A holding the ball in the same hand as Mr B?

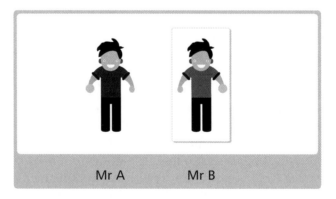

Figure 2.2 Visual–spatial working memory

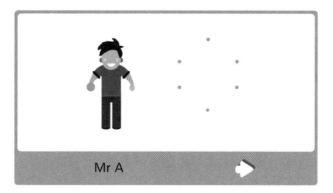

Now touch the location of Mr A's ball on the compass in Figure 2.3.

Mr A

Figure 2.3 Visual–spatial working memory (cont'd)

The tests in the AWMA begin with one item, as you see here. If the individual is successful, more items are added and they have to remember two or more letters and ball locations in the correct sequence.

Assessment: A key feature of standardized assessments is that they are both reliable and valid. This gives the test administrator confidence that the instrument is accurately measuring what it should.

Valid: *Predictive validity* is the ability of a test to predict a certain outcome, such as grades. As research has established that working memory is linked to learning, predictive validity for the AWMA means that a student with a low working memory score would also have poor grades. A large-scale research study of over 3000 students confirmed this pattern: the majority of students with poor working memory also scored poorly on standardized tests of language, math, and vocabulary (Alloway et al., 2009a).

Scores on the AWMA can also identify those who need extra support in the classroom throughout their academic career. Scientific studies demonstrate that working memory predicts success in the classroom from kindergarten to college, and across the range of subjects, from language to maths, from history to art (Cowan and Alloway, 2008). The predictive link between the AWMA and learning is a pattern found not just in typically developing students, but in those with learning disorders, as well as in gifted populations.

Reliable: The AWMA is a '*reliable*' measure of working memory. Reliability refers to the consistency with which a test can reproduce a similar result when used more than once. If an individual gets very different scores when tested at different times, it means that the test is not reliable. If an individual gets similar scores when they take it more than once, the test is reliable. To determine reliability, hundreds of students have been tested and then re-tested on the AWMA between 6 weeks and even 1 year apart. The students had very similar scores when they retook the AWMA, indicating that AWMA produces consistent working memory scores (Alloway et al., 2008b).

Culture-fair: An important feature of the working memory tests in the AWMA is that scores are relatively impervious to environmental factors, such as years of preschool education and socio-economic status (SES), which impact knowledge-based tests. In contrast, working memory measures our **ability** to learn, rather than what we have already learned. The tests are not knowledge-driven and so offer a 'pure' measure of a student's potential to learn.

As part of a government-funded study, hundreds of kindergarteners (5- to 6-year-olds) were tested on a range of cognitive tests, including working memory. We were also interested in how long a child spent in preschool before starting school. Children who attend preschool acquire basic learning blocks, like colors, numbers, letters, even how to spell their name. Would children who spent longer in preschool have better working memory as a result of this exposure to learning? Surprisingly, the study revealed that preschool attendance did not make a difference to working memory scores (Alloway et al., 2004, 2005).

Now let's look at another important factor: socio-economic status (SES). A commonly used index to measure SES is a mother's educational level. Remember Andrew in Chapter 1 – would his working memory scores be different if his mother had a PhD compared to if she left school early with no formal qualifications? When it comes to IQ scores, maternal education makes a difference: children whose parents have a college degree perform better on IQ tests compared to those whose parents left school early with no formal qualifications. Here is why: parents who are well educated are more likely to teach their children more. The more they teach them, the more they are able to learn and the more likely they will do well on an IQ test, which is typically knowledge-based.

In the same study (Alloway et al., 2004), parents were asked to indicate their highest educational level to assess whether this impacts working memory scores. Here again the result was surprising: unlike IQ, working memory scores appear not to be linked to maternal education.

This means that regardless of background or environmental influence, children can have a similar potential to learn.

Let's look more directly at whether financial background influences working memory. Think of a classroom in an underprivileged area in Brazil. There is so much working against these students. Less than 15% finish elementary school. Most leave without learning to read. Schools can't afford to pay their teachers much and the teachers that do stay don't always have the skills and training. But could these students have the same ability and potential as their higher-income peers? A group of colleagues decided to test this theory (Engel et al., 2008). They tested low- and high-income students in Brazil using a Portuguese translation of the AWMA, as well as a verbal ability test. The high-SES students excelled in the verbal ability test where they had to match words with the correct definitions. They superseded their low-SES counterparts in their knowledge, because they had more experience using the words on the test. But they were no better than their low-SES peers on the AWMA.

Dutch colleagues (Messer et al., 2010) found a similar pattern when they investigated differences between immigrant students that typically reside in low-income areas (indexed by parental educational) and comparatively wealthier native language speakers. They found that the low-income immigrant students performed at the same level as their native language peers in the AWMA when tested in their own language. In our own research, we found that socio-economic background also did not impact working memory scores when British students from wealthy backgrounds were compared with their peers from underprivileged backgrounds (Alloway et al., 2014). The general pattern across these studies from different countries is that working memory tests are culture-fair and capture a student's potential to learn.

Working Memory Rating Scale (WMRS)

Teachers can often recognize that something is wrong with a student's working memory and it is useful to have a quick and objective confirmation of the student's working memory profile. The Working Memory Rating Scale (WMRS) is a checklist developed for educators so they can easily identify a student with working memory deficits based on their classroom behavior. It consists of 20 descriptions of behaviors characteristic of students with working memory deficits. Example items include 'Abandons activities before completion' and 'Forgets how to continue an activity that was previously started, despite teacher explanation'. Teachers rate how typical each behavior is of a particular child, using a

4-point scale ranging from 0 (not typical at all) to 1 (occasionally) to 2 (fairly typical) to 3 (very typical).

A starting point in developing the items in the WMRS was an observational study of students with low working memory but typical scores in IQ tests. These students frequently forgot instructions, struggled to cope with tasks involving simultaneous processing and storage, and lost track of their place in complex tasks. The most common consequence of these failures was that the students abandoned the activity without completing it.

These classroom observations led to a government-funded study that allowed our team to sit in classrooms, observe the students' behaviors, learn from the teacher's 'inside perspective' of the students, and match all this information to the students' cognitive profile. The WMRS is the result of the support and cooperation of schools, teachers, and students. This wonderful abundance of information allowed the types of behaviors that were consistently linked to working memory problems to be identified and refined.

Early screener: As the WMRS focuses solely on working-memory-related problems in a single scale, it does not require any training in psychometric assessment prior to use. It is valuable not only as a screening tool for identifying students at risk of poor working memory, but also in illustrating both the classroom situations in which working memory failures frequently arise and the profile of difficulties typically faced by students with poor working memory.

Age-based norms: The scores are normed for each age group, which means that they are representative of typical classroom behavior for each age group. One item in the WMRS is 'Needs regular reminders of each step in the written task'. The classroom teacher has to rate how often the student displays this behavior and then compare their score to the look-up table in the manual. A 5-year-old would need more reminders than a 10-year-old, which is reflected in the scoring of the WMRS.

Easy scoring: The norms in the look-up table are color-coded to make it easy to interpret the results. For example, a score in the green range indicates that it is unlikely that the student has a working memory impairment. If a student's score falls in the yellow range, their behavior suggests some working memory difficulty and that further assessment is recommended. Scores in the red range indicate that the student is manifesting behaviors associated with a working memory problem and targeted support is recommended.

Valid: The WMRS has been validated against other behavior rating scales, such as the Conners' Teacher Rating Scale and the Behavior

Rating Inventory of Executive Function, in order to ensure that it is effective in identifying working memory problems rather than other behavior-based difficulties. Results show that the WMRS measures behaviors that are different from ADHD-type behaviors, and thus reliably identifies students with poor working memory (Alloway et al., 2010b).

The WMRS has also been compared to cognitive tests of working memory (including the AWMA), IQ, and academic attainment. The majority of students identified using the WMRS are more likely to have low working memory scores and achieve low grades (Alloway et al., 2010a). The WMRS provides a valuable tool in detecting working memory deficits so that targeted support can be implemented.

Diagnosis using other standardized tests

As a testament to the growing recognition of the importance of working memory in learning, many standardized test batteries now include assessments of working memory in their repertoire. Discussed here are the working memory tests in a few widely used assessment batteries that you will likely have come across as an educator.

Wechsler Intelligence Scale for Children (WISC)

The Wechsler Intelligence Scale for Children (WISC) is a standardized assessment of cognitive abilities in students aged 6 to 16 years; revised versions include the Working Memory Index. One major limitation of the Working Memory Index is the heavy reliance on verbal information. The student with weak verbal skills may perform poorly simply because of the format of the material, and not because of working memory problems. Furthermore, the student may have visual–spatial working memory strengths that may be undetected by the Working Memory Index in the WISC. Here is a summary of the tests that are included.

Digit Span: The individual hears a sequence of numbers and repeats them in forwards and backwards order. The method of combining forwards digit span with backwards digit span scores conflates verbal short-term memory and verbal working memory. This can artificially raise a student's working memory score as they may do well on the forwards digit span subtest, yet struggle in the backwards digit span subtest.

Letter–Number Sequencing: The individual is presented with a sequence of letters and numbers in mixed order (e.g., T–3–H–7–C–5), and then has to recall the numbers in numerical order and the letters in alphabetical order. This subtest draws heavily on the student's knowledge of number sequencing and the alphabet. Students may perform poorly on this subtest because they have not mastered the alphabet or number sequencing, rather than as a result of working memory problems.

Arithmetic: The supplementary test, which is composed of mental math questions, can also be calculated into the Working Memory Index. However, this test may not directly measure working memory because it conflates math skills with working memory.

Woodcock–Johnson Tests of Cognitive Abilities (WJ Cog)

The WJ Cog is another commonly used test, particularly in North America, to assess cognitive abilities. There are three subtests that measure working memory.

Numbers Reversed: In this subtest, the individual hears a sequence of numbers (2 to 7) and recalls them in backwards order. As discussed in the previous section, this is a highly validated method to assess working memory. The benefit of this version is that it does not include a 'forwards number' component and so measures verbal working memory exclusively.

Auditory Working Memory: This subtest is similar to the Letter–Number Sequencing subtest in the WISC. The individual listens to a string of words and numbers, like *boy – 1 – 4 – soap – 6*. They have to repeat the words first, followed by the numbers. The correct response to the example given is: *boy – soap – 1 – 4 – 6*. This test is thought to measure both working memory and divided attention, although it does run into similar criticisms leveled at its counterpart in the WISC.

Memory for Words: The individual hears a list of words presented verbally and has to repeat them in the same order. This test measures short-term memory, rather than working memory, and a student might do well because they can recall the information, but may not be able to process it.

Understanding standard scores

The test batteries described in this chapter provide the test administrator with standard scores and percentiles. Standard scores are a way of describing a student's performance relative to the performance of others in the same age band. For example, if you are testing a child aged 5 years and 4 months, their performance will be compared with other children aged between 5:0 and 5:11 years. Most students will receive a standard score in the average range. A standard score of more than 130 is extremely high, while a standard score of less than 70 is extremely low; a very small number of students will score at these extremes.

- Standard scores less than 85: below average
- Standard scores between 85 and 115: average
- Standard scores greater than 115: above average

How do these scores translate to classroom support? If a student has a score that is below average (less than 85), this is an indication of a working memory deficit that will lead to learning difficulties. As a result, these students may have access to special education services and accommodations, such as curriculum modification. Schools that conduct whole-class screening using the AWMA are able to tailor the curriculum according to the students' working memory strengths and weaknesses.

A team approach

Now that you have identified a student with poor working memory, what happens next? The first step is to create whole-school awareness. It is always wonderful when a classroom teacher recognizes the student's needs and works to support them. How frustrating then for the student when they move to a different teacher who is unaware of their difficulties. It is important to foster an environment where both the teachers and the students are aware of the individual's learning needs and where what works for the student is shared with their next teacher.

Educators can work together with psychologists and clinicians to provide an accurate and comprehensive approach to diagnosis and support. In all of the learning disorders addressed in this book, teachers cannot diagnose the problem, whether it is dyslexia, DCD, ADHD, autistic spectrum disorder, or an anxiety disorder. However, teachers are in a unique position to evaluate the student's behavior in the classroom and how their difficulty impacts on their learning. A teacher's role in this process has been described as the eyes and ears for how a child manages with everyday activities. The teacher sees the student on a regular basis and can assess how that student compares with their classmates. This perspective is one that cannot be taken for granted, and ultimately it can determine whether an intervention will be successful.

Summary

1. The Automated Working Memory Assessment (AWMA) is a standard-ized and objective test that provides details on a student's unique verbal and visual–spatial working memory profile.
2. The Working Memory Rating Scale (WMRS) can be used to evaluate classroom behavior and find out if a student is at risk of having poor working memory.
3. Some standardized IQ test batteries include working memory sub-tests as well.

References and further reading

Alloway, T.P. (2007a) *Automated Working Memory Assessment (AWMA)*. London: Psychological Corporation.

Alloway, T.P. (2007b) What can phonological and semantic information tell us about the mechanisms of immediate sentence recall? *Memory*, 15: 605–15.

Alloway, T.P. (2009) Working memory, but not IQ, predicts subsequent learn-ing in children with learning difficulties. *European Journal of Psychological Assessment*, 25: 92–8.

Alloway, T.P. (2011) The benefits of computerized working memory assessment. *Educational & Child Psychology*, 28: 8–17.

Alloway, T.P. and Alloway, R.G. (2013) working memory in the lifespan: a cross-sectional approach. *Journal of Cognitive Psychology*, 25: 84–93.

Alloway, T.P. and Ledwon, F. (2014) Semantic information and working memory in sentence recall in children. *International Journal of Educational Research*, 65: 1–8.

Alloway, T.P., Gathercole, S.E., Willis, C., and Adams, A.M. (2004) A structural analysis of working memory and related cognitive skills in early childhood. *Journal of Experimental Child Psychology*, 87, 85–106.

Alloway, T.P., Gathercole, S.E., Willis, C., and Adams, A.M. (2005). Working memory and special educational needs. *Educational and Child Psychology*, 22: 56–67.

Alloway, T.P., Alloway, R.G., and Wootan, S. (2014) Home sweet home: Does where you live matter to working memory and other cognitive skills? *Journal of Experimental Child Psychology*, 124: 124–31.

Alloway, T.P., Doherty-Sneddon, G., and Forbes, L. (2012) Teachers' perceptions of classroom behavior and working memory. *Education Research & Reviews*, 7: 138–42.

Alloway, T.P., Gathercole, S.E., and Elliott, J. (2010a) Examining the link between working memory behavior and academic attainment in children with ADHD. *Developmental Medicine & Child Neurology*, 52: 632–6.

Alloway, T.P., Elliott, J., and Place, M. (2010b). Investigating the relationship between attention and working memory in clinical and community samples. *Child Neuropsychology*, 16: 242–54.

Alloway, T.P., Gathercole, S.E., and Kirkwood, H. (2008a) *Working Memory Rating Scale*. London: Psychological Corporation.

Alloway, T.P., Gathercole, S.E, Kirkwood, H.J., and Elliott, J.E. (2008b) Evaluating the validity of the Automated Working Memory Assessment. *Educational Psychology*, 7: 725–34.

Alloway, T.P., Gathercole, S.E, Kirkwood, H.J., and Elliott, J.E. (2009a) The cognitive and behavioral characteristics of children with low working memory. *Child Development*, 80: 606–21.

Alloway, T.P., Gathercole, S., Kirkwood, H., and Elliott, J. (2009b) The Working Memory Rating Scale: a classroom-based behavioral assessment of WM. *Learning & Individual Differences*, 19: 242–5.

Alloway, T.P., Gathercole, S., Holmes, J., Place, M., and Elliott, J. (2009c) The diagnostic utility of behavioral checklists in identifying children with ADHD and children with WM deficits. *Child Psychiatry & Human Development*, 40: 353–66.

Cowan, N. and Alloway, T.P. (2008) The development of working memory in childhood, in M. Courage and N. Cowan (eds), *Development of Memory in Infancy and Childhood*, 2nd edn. Hove: Psychology Press.

Engel, P. M. J., Heloisa Dos Santos, F., and Gathercole, S.E. (2008) Are working memory measures free of socio-economic influence? *Journal of Speech, Language, and Hearing Research*, 51: 1580–7.

Injoque-Ricle, I., Calero, A., Alloway, T.P., and Burin, D. (2011) Assessing WM in Spanish-speaking children: Automated Working Memory Assessment battery adaptation. *Learning & Individual Differences*, 21: 78–84.

Messer, M.H., Leseman, P.P.M., Mayo, A.Y. and Boom, J. (2010) Long-term phonotactic knowledge supports verbal short-term memory in young native and second language learners. *Journal of Experimental Child Psychology*, 105: 306–23.

CHAPTER 3

SPECIFIC LEARNING DISORDER: READING DIFFICULTIES (DYSLEXIA)

This chapter looks at:

- WHAT are reading difficulties?
- WHERE are the affected brain regions?
- WHY is working memory linked to reading difficulties?
- HOW can working memory be supported in students with reading difficulties?

Jane was well liked by everyone and always had witty answers to hand when asked a question. But, when expected to put her thoughts to paper, she struggled. During one group project on the topic of 'whale hunting', she led the discussion and convinced the class that the practice should be outlawed by drawing on statistics showing declining populations, as well as an ethical argument based on whale conservation, demonstrating her intelligence and emotion. Though her presentation was excellent, the written portion of the project seemed as if a different student had written it: the argument on paper was out of sequence and incoherent; sentences were short, with many misspelled words;

the ideas were very simplistic, with none of the flair and complexity of Jane's classroom discussion. Her teacher was at a loss to explain the contrast between her oral and written arguments. But it was a typical result for Jane, and he had to mark a project that was on track for an 'A', with a 'C' instead.

You wouldn't know it from speaking to her, but Jane has reading difficulties, commonly referred to as *dyslexia*. In this chapter, we use the terms 'reading difficulties' and 'dyslexia' interchangeably. Depending on how often you listen to your students' conversations, you may not be aware that they have reading difficulties. But if you have ever graded something that looks like it was written by a student two grade levels below the one you teach, chances are that the student may have a reading difficulty.

WHAT it is

According to the International Dyslexia Association, dyslexia is a specific learning disability characterized by unexpected difficulties in accurate and/or fluent word recognition, decoding, and spelling. Younger students with dyslexia tend to struggle more with sounds, than the meaning of words. This can explain why students with dyslexia are often described as bright and articulate, yet their written work shows little evidence of this.

Students with dyslexia show deficits in *phonological awareness*, an important building block for reading. Phonological awareness is ability to connect letters to sounds. It means that you know the letter 'c' makes the sound /k/, 'a' makes the sound /æ/, and 't' makes the sound /t/. By knowing the sounds that letters make, you can know what the collection of letters mean, for example that 'c', 'a', and 't', combine to make the word 'cat'. Phonological awareness is like a decoder ring that helps you decrypt the letters on the page. Without phonological awareness, reading is like trying to make sense of unintelligible hieroglyphics. In a 5-year longitudinal study of several hundred children who were followed from kindergarten through fourth grade (5- to 10-year-olds), phonological awareness skills predicted the students' reading ability (Wagner and Muse, 2006; also Wagner et al., 1994).

Typically, developing readers have an automatized internal look-up table of phonemes that they use in writing. Some students with dyslexia can write and spell longer words provided that they are phonetically regular. However, these students' difficulty becomes apparent with phonetically irregular words, and this is evident in their riting. Did you spot the spelling error for 'writing' in the previous sentence? Such errors are common in the work of students with dyslexia, who rely on spelling phonetically (like 'laf' instead of 'laugh').

Try It: Phonological awareness

Individuals with dyslexia often have difficulty in understanding the sound structures of words. In particular, they struggle in a skill known as segmentation and blending: breaking up words into smaller segments (example: *c* from *–at*) and putting them together. This skill is tested using 'spoonerisms', where you exchange the first sound unit in each word.

Example: *fat dog = dat fog*

Here are some more – see how quickly you can do them (answers are below):

- cat flap
- bad salad
- soap in your hole
- mean as custard
- plaster man
- chewing the doors

(*Answers*: flat cap, sad ballad, hope in your soul, keen as mustard, master plan, doing the chores.)

You can try some of these phonological awareness tasks with your students. They are similar to some of the standardized tests that psychologists can use to identify dyslexia:

- Rhyming games: Do *cat* and *bat* end in the same sound?
- Phoneme elision (pronouncing a word after leaving out the first or the last sound). Example: Say the word *cup*. Now tell me what word would be left if I said *cup* without saying /k/.
- Sound categorization: Find the odd one out in sets of words such as *fun, bun, pin, ton*.
- Phoneme segmentation: Tell me each sound you hear in the word in the order that you hear it.
- Blending phonemes into words.

DSM and diagnosis

There has been a shift in the *DSM-5* criteria so dyslexia now falls under an umbrella category known as specific learning disorder. The focus of this diagnosis is on general academic achievement, which incorporates a range of deficits that influence academic achievement, including reading, math, and writing.

There is also no longer a strict requirement to use a discrepancy criterion to identify reading difficulties (difference between average IQ score and low reading score). Some psychologists favor standardized test batteries that assess a range of cognitive skills associated with reading difficulty, such as phonological awareness, verbal working memory, auditory processing, and rapid naming skills. Such test batteries are useful as they reveal specific areas of deficits in reading skills. Reading performance of many students with dyslexia is often two to three grade levels lower than their peers.

WHERE it is: Working memory and reading in the brain

At first glance, the role of working memory in the dyslexic brain doesn't make much sense. Brain scans show that in most learning disorders, the prefrontal cortex (PFC), the brain region that is the home of WM, has less activation compared to the PFCs of those without the learning disorders. Less blood in the PFC can mean that working memory is not working as hard.

But dyslexia is unusual. Brain scans of students with dyslexia actually show the opposite. Their PFC shows more activation compared to those that don't have dyslexia (Shaywitz et al., 2002, 2003). When students with dyslexia read or perform tasks associated with reading, their working memory is working harder than when students without dyslexia perform those same tasks. This is the case for even the most basic of reading skills. In one study, those with dyslexia and those without it were asked if letters like 't' and 'v' rhymed. Researchers found that students with dyslexia had greater activation in the PFC compared to those without it.

Does this mean that working memory is in fact a strength rather than a weakness for those with dyslexia? Yes and no. Students with dyslexia also have less blood flowing to the language areas of the brain compared with students without dyslexia. These areas are responsible for our ability to connect the letters we read with the sounds they make. Because these areas aren't working as hard, a student with dyslexia struggles to recognize the words they are reading.

It also means that their working memory has to step in and fill the gap left by the underperforming language areas of the brain. But this is hard for working memory to do. It is like being in a three-legged race, but your partner isn't jumping or running as fast as you, so you have to use extra strength to make it across the finish line.

For students without dyslexia, skills associated with reading are more automatized and require less effort to accomplish. But, for those with dyslexia, they have to work harder to accomplish the same task. When they are reading simple sentences, with easy-to-understand words and concepts, this isn't so much of a problem. But they begin to struggle when the text is more complex and challenging than they are used to. Working memory is so busy trying to read each unfamiliar word that it can't help the reader understand what they are reading. To illustrate our point, try reading an unfamiliar text with unfamiliar words. Try reading the following lines from Chaucer's *Canterbury Tales*, written in Middle English.

Whan that Aprill with his shoures soote

The droghte of March hath perced to the roote,

And bathed every veyne in swich licour

Of which vertu engendred is the flour,

Whan Zephirus eek with his sweete breeth

Inspired hath in every holt and heeth

The tendre croppes, and the yonge sonne ...

Making sense of these lines on the first reading is anything but automatic (unless, of course, you just taught your students Chaucer!). The language areas in the brain and working memory have to work together just to make sense of the words. For example, your working memory and your language areas help you realize that 'whan' means 'when', 'yonge' is 'young', and 'soote' means 'sweet'. But because you are focusing your working memory on making sense of the words, it is much harder to figure out what the lines mean. Now let's look at a more modern English translation of the same lines:

When April with his showers sweet with fruit

The drought of March has pierced unto the root

And bathed each vein with liquor that has power

To generate therein and sire the flower;

When Zephyr also has, with his sweet breath,

Quickened again, in every holt and heath,

The tender shoots and buds, and the young sun …

Because the words in the modern version are familiar ('when' is actually spelled 'when'), the language areas of the brain automatically recognize the words, and working memory is freed up to make sense of the syntax and meaning of the poem. This reading is much easier, as working memory helps you understand that the lines mean that April rains make plants bloom, and Chaucer was referring to Springtime. For students with dyslexia, every time they read something unfamiliar, it is like reading Chaucer – they spend so much effort reading the words themselves that they can't make sense of the meaning of the text.

WHY working memory is linked to dyslexia

Science Flash: Is it all in the eyes?

There has been much made of eye movement patterns of dyslexic readers. Their eyes often move erratically up and down a page rather than smoothly across a page like those of typically developing readers. But do their eye movements lead to difficulties in reading or are their eye movements a result of their difficulties? One study set out to find the answer.

Psychologists tracked the eye movements of typically developing readers while they were reading material that was too difficult for them. In contrast, students with dyslexia were asked to read easy texts.

Now the eye movements of the typically developing readers were unpredictable and moved up and down the page. In contrast, eye movements of the students with dyslexia looked like typical readers. This study, and many others like it, provides strong evidence that the erratic eye movements observed in the students with dyslexia are a *symptom*, not the cause, of reading difficulties (Hutzler et al., 2006).

Individuals with dyslexia show marked decrements in verbal working memory (see Figure 3.1). This deficit is present in childhood, but may taper off by adulthood.

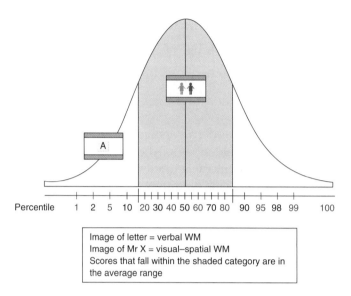

Percentile   1   2   5   10   20 30 40 50 60 70 80   90 95 98 99   100

Image of letter = verbal WM
Image of Mr X = visual–spatial WM
Scores that fall within the shaded category are in
the average range

Figure 3.1   Working memory profile of reading difficulties

Working memory and dyslexia in the early years

In young children, their poor verbal working memory makes it harder for them to learn and automatize highly familiar words, and thus it takes them longer to learn them. One behavior pattern as a result of this is seeing mirror images of words or letters: reading 'was' as 'saw', or confusing the letters 'b' and 'd'. However, it is important to note that these errors are not unique to dyslexia: normal beginner readers also make such errors. Researchers have argued that the way we read from left to right in English is arbitrary, must be learned, and can result in confusion in early readers. Letter pairs, such as 'b' and 'd' are confusing both visually and verbally (because they are both *stop consonants*) for beginner readers too. In fact, when students with dyslexia are matched with normal readers on the same reading level (i.e., younger children), both groups make similar reversal errors with letters and words. Thus, the reading patterns of a student with dyslexia mimic a beginner reader.

Working memory and dyslexia in middle childhood

Case Study: David

My son David is 10 and he is very bright, but his main problem is his difficulty in writing things down. He says the problem is finding the words, especially the first word. He takes forever to write down a very short story, and is usually disappointed with it because he has a much more complex vision of the story in his head (like a movie) but cannot get to the words to write it down. The less processing that is involved, such as figuring out where to start and which details to include, the quicker he can write. For example, writing down a set of instructions for how to make a sandwich would be done faster than a story (still slower than average). He is very quiet in groups, cannot take in more than a few verbal instructions at once, often forgets what he is sent to do, often fails to start a task until reminded, often seems to be daydreaming, and has problems organizing himself to do something. He drives me and his teacher mad with the need for constant reminders of what he is supposed to be doing.

Students with dyslexia, like David, have very poor verbal (auditory) working memory and they have difficulty remembering the sequence of information that is presented out loud, such as instructions, new vocabulary words, and even names. Their poor verbal working memory means that they have a hard time repeating new or unfamiliar verbal information. This can make them embarrassed to repeat information in front of others.

It takes considerable working memory space to keep in mind the relevant speech sounds and concepts necessary for identifying words and understanding text, which can exceed the capacity of the student with dyslexia. Thus, the combination of processing and remembering verbal information, rather than just remembering information, is very difficult for the individual with dyslexia. This happened to David when he was writing his story: the more information he had to process when writing the story, the longer it took him to complete the activity.

When it comes to writing, students need both verbal working memory and phonological awareness skills to blend the phonemes of a word, combine words to make a meaningful sentence, and finally remember what they want to say in order to write it down. David struggled to translate his visual image of a story to paper because his working memory was not big enough to combine these elements and then translate them to paper.

There are several reasons why students with reading difficulties have such poor verbal working memory skills. One explanation is that they have difficulty in repeating the information fast enough to remember it. Most of us rehearse information to prevent memory loss, at least until we get a pen and paper. The speed with which we rehearse information is linked to how much information we can hold in working memory. However, it takes the individual with dyslexia much longer to repeat phrases and, as a result, they can run out of time to rehearse all the important information. Here is an example: if you give your class a list of five things to do on their way back to their desk, the student with dyslexia may only have time to repeat two of those five things, and thus be more likely to leave some of the tasks unfinished.

The way in which they rehearse information is also important: the student has to repeat all the information in the correct sequence, starting from the beginning of the list to the end. However, the student with dyslexia is unlikely to repeat information this way. Let's go back to the example of the five instructions: the student with dyslexia will start rehearsing from the *end of the list* and consequently they tend to forget all but the last bit of information they heard.

Students with dyslexia have **strengths** in visual–spatial working memory. Studies comparing visual memory for novel objects confirm that students with dyslexia perform similarly to normal readers. However, if students with dyslexia are asked to label the objects, their performance drops because they have to rely on verbal working memory. Their good visual working memory means that they learn words as a unit, rather than work out their individual sounds. This strategy can be quite useful initially as they build up an impressive mental look-up table. But they usually find new words very difficult, as they do not have the skills to match the sounds to the letters to decipher them. For example, they may be able to quickly read the word 'hawk' if it was part of their look-up table, but the word 'tomahawk' would be hard to read if it was unfamiliar to them.

Working memory and dyslexia in adulthood

Some researchers suggest that there is a shift in the deficits driving reading difficulties from childhood to adulthood. While children with dyslexia find it hard to process the sounds of the word, adults with dyslexia struggle more with integrating the sounds with the meanings of the words.

There is great heterogeneity in the adult dyslexic profile. In some cases, there can be a working memory deficit, while in other adults with dyslexia their working memory may be in the average range. In one research article that examined over 50 studies, Swanson (2012) suggested that verbal working memory underpins other processes related to reading, and acts as a compensatory mechanism for other deficiencies. As discussed previously, working memory is involved in keeping multiple pieces of information in mind, such as matching the words on the page with the appropriate sounds, and then combining the words to comprehend what they read. If some information is not automatized, such as the individual unit sounds, working memory could be recruited to break down each word into smaller units before they can read it. As a result, working memory resources could be used both for lower-level processes like reading the individual words, as well as higher-level processes, like putting the words together to understand the meaning of a sentence, thereby taxing an already overworked working memory.

However, in some cases adults may not even show any evidence of working memory deficits. For example, research comparing working memory skills of college students with reading difficulties and those with normal reading skills (Alloway et al., 2014) revealed that those with dyslexia performed similarly in the working memory tests compared to the normal readers. It is possible that these adults did not demonstrate any working memory deficits because they had developed their phonological skills well enough not to require working memory. Furthermore, as this was a sample of college students, it may be that since they were successful enough to attend college, they had developed coping mechanisms that did not put a burden on their working memory.

HOW: Strategies to support working memory

Two types of strategies are discussed here: **general working memory strategies** that can be applied to students with general learning needs, and **specific working memory strategies** for students with dyslexia. While the general strategies below are tailored for those with reading difficulties, you can modify them as appropriate for other students in your classroom.

General strategies

Use visual representation to support working memory. The strategy relies on the dyslexic student's strength: visual–spatial working memory. As students with dyslexia have reading difficulties, the use of visual representation supports their learning. One 13-year-old boy with dyslexia drew an amazing picture of a Minotaur and filled it with dates and events so he could visualize facts from his Latin class. Anne, a Scottish teacher, made her student a visual picture strip to teach him initial sound blends. This reduced the working memory load, and the student was able to focus on identifying which two out of three words began with the same blend.

Reduce working memory processing in activities. Present information in a different way to reduce the working memory processing. James, a history teacher in Colorado, says he has dyslexia. So when he teaches history dates, he finds it easier to present them vertically (straight down the page), rather than horizontally. The vertical presentation of information makes it easier for students with dyslexia to process as it is easier for them to visualize the information.

Study guides and outlines of notes are also useful in helping the student follow along during a classroom lesson. These are useful in identifying the main idea of the lesson. Examples that illustrate connections between ideas, or link new information to existing knowledge, can help the student with dyslexia use their working memory to retain the lesson, rather than keep up with the lesson.

Keep track of their place in complex activities. In reading, the younger student with dyslexia often spends a long time trying to decipher an unfamiliar word and falls behind as a result. The older student will likely skip over an unfamiliar word as they do not want to spend the time deciphering it. By the time they reach the end of the paragraph, they have skipped over so many words that they are unable to make sense of the text.

When they come to an unfamiliar word, encourage the student to put a dot under the word (with pencil if you do not want to mark up the book), and then return to that word after they finish reading. They can also use a ruler to keep track of their place when reading.

Specific strategies

Automatize letters and word components. Students with dyslexia often struggle with recognizing letters and word components (like 'er' or 'ight'), forcing them to use their limited working memory capacity to reconstruct sounds. This means that they have little working memory space left over to comprehend what they are reading, for example in determining the definition of words, or in the meaning of the sentence and paragraph.

Early years strategy. Younger students with dyslexia can save their working memory resources for comprehension by familiarizing letter and word recognition. Get a page from a book, magazine, or newspaper. Ask them to circle all the 't's on a page, all the 'er's, all the 'ought's, etc. Focus on one letter or word ending at a time and build up progressively as they demonstrate mastery of the letter or word component. Don't jump ahead until they can consistently circle all the targeted text.

Increase working memory processing. Older students with dyslexia often recruit working memory to read a text, leaving them very little working memory resources to comprehend that text. One way to increase their working memory speed is to give them easy passages to read and ask them to speed-read them. This exercise will increase their ability to speed-read words, as well as increase their confidence in reading.

Speak slowly to reduce working memory processing. Students with dyslexia take longer to process information, so speaking quickly can hinder their ability to remember the entire set of instructions. Remind yourself to speak slowly. This is especially true if you have been teaching for a while. You may have taught the lesson many times before, but your students are hearing it for the first time.

Record instructions to reduce working memory processing. Students with dyslexia commonly have great oral communication skills. However, there is often a disparity between their speech and their written work. By recording what they want to say before writing it down, students with dyslexia can formulate their ideas and plan their essay so their written work matches their oral skills.

Rehearse to keep information active. Students with dyslexia often forget things at the beginning of the list.

Early years strategy. Ask them to start at the beginning of the list and say each item out aloud in the correct sequence. While the older student will eventually feel comfortable repeating information in their head, the younger student may benefit from moving their mouth and speaking quietly.

Shorten activities to reduce the working memory load. Individuals with dyslexia struggle to complete tasks on time because they spend a lot of mental effort processing the activity. Reduce working memory processing by giving them a shorter activity. For older students, give them shorter assignments. If the homework is 20 multiplication problems, the student with dyslexia can complete 10 or 12 problems instead. This will allow them to master the concept of the lesson without being frustrated that it took so much effort to process each sum.

Early years strategy. Mary was teaching her 6-year-old class the concept of *first*, *third*, and *last* using a line of 10 flowers. She presented each idea step by step and then modeled what the student had to do: color in the relevant flowers in the line. Yet, Sam still wasn't able to follow along, and randomly colored the flowers. Mary decided to give him an activity sheet with five flowers and repeated the instructions just for him. He was quickly able to learn the concepts and could follow along when the class moved on to learning the concepts of *second*, *fourth*, and *fifth* the following week.

Make information concrete to reduce working memory processing. Give students something concrete to make it easier for them to keep track of their place in a multi-step activity. Use numbers instead of bullet points, or with younger children use different colors instead.

Current Debate: Is reading instruction linked to reading difficulties?

Does learning to read holistically – where the reader is expected to recognize the word by its visual characteristics – cultivate reading difficulties? Reading holistically refers to focusing on the way the word looks. Does it have a dangling bit or an upright part? Early readers have to create a huge database of words that they know by 'sight'. Audio books on tape also encourage this method of reading as the child hears the word and matches it with what is on the page.

While initially the child may feel a sense of achievement in being able to read, some experts think that holistic instruction damages reading skills and ultimately contributes to reading difficulties. Sight-reading depends on a good memory as the child needs to keep adding new words to the mental database. In the classroom, new words can be taught at a pace that is too fast for the student with dyslexia and so they cannot keep up and end up lagging behind their classmates.

Sight-reading also does not give the child tools for reading, unlike phonetic learning. In phonetic instruction, the child is taught that each letter is matched with a sound and so gives them skills to decipher new words on their own by 'sounding it out'. Given the importance of phonological awareness and verbal working memory, some educators suggest that we should revisit the phonics method of reading instruction.

Case Study: Rebecca

Rebecca, 16 years old, was in her junior year at a public high school. She was very popular and was involved with many extra-curricular activities, primarily sports. She began in my elective class, music appreciation, and I noticed a problem almost immediately. My class requires reading music, historical texts, and writing. We had an assignment that required students to use a song-writing program, as well as write a short essay on the inspiration behind the song they composed. The song-writing program sings the notes that the students put into it, so they did not need any in-depth musical knowledge. Rebecca excelled at the song composition, but she did very poorly in her essay-writing assignment.

The assignment should have taken an hour to complete, but Rebecca needed an extension for her work. She turned in the writing portion the next day but it was filled with errors. For example, her sentences were jumbled; instead of saying 'My mother was my inspiration for this song' she wrote 'Mother my song was inspiration for this'.

Another issue was doing multiple assignments at the same time. I often gave students a piece of music to translate into notes, a reading assignment based on the musical piece, and a written essay. Rebecca was often confused about which assignment came first, and what she had to do for each one. She also spent a great amount of time reading the assigned text.

Strategies

- Shorten activities to reduce the working memory load

I began reordering my lesson plan to better accommodate Rebecca's pace. Instead of giving three assignments at once, I gave one assignment first, and when students completed it, I handed them the next one.

- Make information concrete to reduce working memory processing

Instead of just verbalizing the instructions for the class, I wrote them on the board, numbering them in order of completion. For instance: '#1 Write a song using a trumpet, #2 Read a story about Chuck Mangione, and #3 Write three interesting facts you learned about him.' This made it easier for Rebecca to keep track of what she needed to accomplish.

- Reduce working memory processing in activities

Since Rebecca's biggest difficulty was in reading, I offered her taped versions of the reading assignments. This allowed her to keep up with the class and complete all the activities.

- Break down information to reduce working memory processing

I also broke down the essay into small two-sentence chunks for Rebecca. Instead of a long essay assignment, I asked smaller questions. For instance, for the essay topic 'Briefly explain who Louis Armstrong was, and provide some interesting facts about his career and life', I broke it into: 'Who was Louis Armstrong?', 'What instrument did Louis Armstrong play?', 'List one interesting fact about Louis Armstrong'. These questions related to the requirements of the essay, yet allowed Rebecca to take smaller steps to complete the assignment.

I also broke down larger words like 'monotone' into smaller units – 'mono' and 'tone' – so Rebecca could recognize them and understand what they meant. I found that breaking down the tasks, and even words, dramatically improved her performance in my class.

Case Study: Jared

Jared is a 9-year-old boy in my 4th grade class. Although he appears to be well-adjusted, he has very low self-esteem when it comes to school-work. He has been struggling over the last few weeks, but his performance is not weak enough for him to enter a slower-paced class. While teaching, I catch him zoning out, staring at the trees outside of our class window. Because of his inattention, he struggles in class. While most of his classmates can demonstrate the process they followed to solve a math problem, Jared cannot. When I observed him one day, I noticed that he used his fingers to count, rather than write down the steps. For instance, for the problem '10 x 8', he counted by tens using his fingers: '10, 20, 30, 40, ...' until he reached the answer '80'.

Jared finds reading assignments a challenge as well. He becomes frustrated during them, often complaining that his desk is moving and that he cannot focus on the writing. He tells me that he gets stomach aches and headaches while trying to read. He spends 30 minutes on a single page and when asked to read aloud, he often reads the same lines multiple times or skips over lines.

Strategies

- Minimize distractions so working memory is not overwhelmed

Jared needed individualized attention, so I decided to move his desk to the front of the class, farthest away from the windows and the door. After doing this, he was better able to focus on the lesson when I was teaching.

- Break down information to reduce working memory processing

I gave Jared step-by-step instructions to solve math problems on paper. I took a problem such as '10 x 8' and asked him to write the problem like '10 over 8'. Then he would multiply the '8' by the '0' of '10' then multiply the '8' again by the '1'. The result was '80' and I could see that he followed the steps as instructed in class, rather than use his fingers. This method allowed him to solve more complex math problems using the same steps. When reading, I asked him to read two sentences at a time, then three, and so on, until he was able to read a whole page at a time.

- Keep track of place in complex activities

When Jared was reading, I gave him a popsicle stick to use so he could follow along on the page. This wooden stick underlined each word as he was reading so he would not make the mistake of re-reading the same sentence again, or skip over a sentence.

- Shorten activities to reduce the working memory load

Jared often got motion sickness while he read, as he thought his desk was moving, though it was not. To combat this, we took reading breaks where we discussed the information he had just read. This drastically reduced the incidences of headaches and gave him time to process and retain the information he had just read.

Summary

1. **Core deficit**: Students with reading difficulties have difficulty with phonological awareness (learning and discriminating sounds of words), which impacts spelling, reading, and writing.
2. **Working memory profile**: Students with reading difficulties have impairments in *verbal working memory*, but average visual–spatial working memory.
3. **Strategies**: Support these students by giving shorter instructions and activities; and reduce working memory processing in classroom activities.

References and further reading

Alloway, T.P. and Archibald, L.M. (2008) Working memory and learning in children with developmental coordination disorder and specific language impairment. *Journal of Learning Disabilities*, 41: 251–62.

Alloway, T.P. and Gathercole, S.E. (2005) The role of sentence recall in reading and language skills of children with learning difficulties. *Learning and Individual Differences*, 15: 271–82.

Alloway, T.P. and Gregory, D. (2013) The predictive ability of IQ and working memory scores in literacy in an adult population. *International Journal of Educational Research*, 57: 51–6.

Alloway, T.P., Wootan, S., and Deane, P. (2014) Investigating working memory and sustained attention in dyslexic adults. *International Journal of Educational Research,* 67: 11–17.

Berninger, V.W., Raskind, W., Richards, T., Abbott, R., and Stock, P. (2008) A multidisciplinary approach to understanding developmental dyslexia within working-memory architecture: genotypes, phenotypes, brain, and instruction. *Developmental Neuropsychology*, 33: 707–44.

Gathercole, S.E., Alloway, T.P., Willis, C., and Adams, A.M. (2006) Working memory in children with reading disabilities. *Journal of Experimental Child Psychology*, 93: 265–81.

Hutzler, F., Kronbichler, M., Jacobs, A.M., and Wimmer, H. (2006) Perhaps correlational but not causal: no effect of dyslexic readers' magnocellular system on their eye movements during reading. *Neuropsychologia*, 44: 637–48.

Savage, R., Lavers, N., and Pillay, V. (2007) Working memory and reading difficulties: what we know and what we don't know about the relationship. *Educational Psychology Review*, 19: 185–221.

Shaywitz, B., Shaywitz, S., Pugh, K., Mencl, W., Fulbright, R., Skudlarski, P., et al. (2002) Disruption of posterior brain systems for reading in children with developmental dyslexia. *Biological Psychiatry*, 52: 101–10.

Shaywitz, S., Shaywitz, B., Fulbright, R., Skudlarski, P., Mencl, W., Constable, R., et al. (2003) Neural systems for compensation and persistence: young adult outcome of childhood reading disability. *Biological Psychiatry*, 54: 25–33.

Swanson, H.L. (2012) Adults with reading disabilities: converting a meta-analysis to practice. *Journal of Learning Disabilities*, 45: 17–30.

Wagner, R.K. and Muse, A. (2006) Working memory deficits in developmental dyslexia, in T.P. Alloway and S.E. Gathercole (eds), *Working Memory in Neurodevelopmental Conditions*. Hove: Psychology Press.

Wagner, R.K., Torgesen, J.K., and Rashotte, C.A. (1994) Development of reading-related phonological processing abilities: new evidence of bidirectional causality from a latent variable longitudinal study. *Developmental Psychology*, 30: 73–87.

CHAPTER 4

SPECIFIC LEARNING DISORDER: MATH DIFFICULTIES (DYSCALCULIA)

This chapter looks at:

- WHAT are math difficulties?
- WHERE are the affected brain regions?
- WHY is working memory linked to math difficulties?
- HOW can working memory be supported in students with math difficulties?

Here are two very similar stories from parents from different parts of the world. Janet from the USA says that her 12-year-old daughter, Madeline, has many problems with learning:

> She remembers so little! For the past three years we have paid for her to have private math lessons. These are only for half an hour once a week because she cannot cope with more than that. She seems to have a mental block with math and has not progressed in the last two years. I think she is turning off, telling herself that she 'cannot do it'.

Another parent, in the UK, writes that her son, Jacob, 10 years old, 'still struggles with simple arithmetic. Learning to tell the time is still slow – he has not mastered "half-past". Although he managed to learn his 5× tables because we practised all summer, this has now gone.'

Both Madeline and Jacob have dyscalculia, a math difficulty where students struggle to learn or understand mathematics. Students with dyscalculia lack foundational number knowledge (or *number sense*) necessary for building subsequent math skills. For example, they often do not know basic number names ('eight' stands for '8' or 'twenty' stands for '20'). They also struggle with number magnitude and cannot tell if a number like 37 is larger or smaller than 28. However, dyscalculia encompasses more than problems with numbers; it also includes difficulty with telling the time (as in Jacob's case), identifying left from right, and recognizing patterns. Scientific understanding of dyscalculia has progressed more slowly than dyslexia, in part because of the complexity of different math skills.

WHAT it is

While students with dyscalculia are able to learn the basic rules for counting, such as counting in a sequence, they find more complex math tasks to be a challenge. The typical child begins to understand math rules when they are 3 to 4 years old and builds on them. For example, they learn that we count in sequence on a horizontal number line, going from left to right. However, this conceptual understanding in the student with dyscalculia can be delayed by one to two years.

Their progress when learning basic arithmetic skills is slower than typical students, which means that they cannot remember as many facts as their peers and also quickly forget them. So when asked to solve simple arithmetic problems like '1 + 3', they cannot complete it without using a strategy, like counting it out on their fingers. However, such strategies are usually time-consuming and inefficient, resulting in errors.

DSM and diagnosis

There has been a shift in the *DSM-5* criteria, so dyscalculia now falls under an umbrella category known as specific learning disorder. The focus of this diagnosis is on general academic achievement, which incorporates a range of deficits that influence academic achievement, including reading, math, and writing.

There is also no longer a strict requirement to use a discrepancy criterion to identify math difficulties (difference between average IQ score and low math score). Some psychologists favor standardized test batteries that assess a range of math skills, such as number sense, mental arithmetic, place values, and fractions. Such test batteries are useful as they reveal specific areas of math deficits.

WHERE it is: Working memory and math in the brain

For typically developing students, solving a math problem is like a beautiful piece of music made possible by an orchestra of musicians, each playing their instrument perfectly. In the brain, the conductor of the music is the prefrontal cortex (PFC), the home of working memory. The PFC works together with other brain regions, like the intraparietal sulcus (IPS) and the angular gyrus, to recognize number magnitude, store math facts, and calculate answers. All these brain areas can work together to solve a math problem (Bugden et al., 2012; Vicario et al., 2012).

But for a student with dyscalculia, the musicians don't play as well and the conductor isn't up to the task of directing them; the combined result is a cacophony. Brain imaging studies show that for students with dyscalculia, important regions like the IPS underperform, and this may underpin their math difficulties. Neuroscientists have also determined that the PFC of children with dyscalculia is different than their peers, suggesting a possible underlying cause for their poor working memory.

WHY working memory is linked to math difficulties

A poor working memory is at the heart of dyscalculia (see Figure 4.1). This makes it harder to memorize math facts and apply them to a math problem. In a large study (Friso-van den Bos et al., 2013) exploring the role of working memory in math across kindergarten to 5th grade (5- to 11-year-olds), the researchers found that the higher a student's working memory, the better their performance on math achievement tests. Visual–spatial working memory in particular predicts how well that children perform in math problems. Visual–spatial memory works like a mental blackboard giving students a space to solve arithmetic tasks.

Typically developing students use their working memory to accumulate a library of math facts, like '8 + 7 = 15', 39 is bigger than 27, and

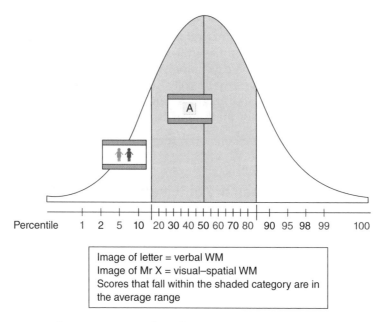

Percentile   1   2   5   10   20 30 40 50 60 70 80   90 95 98 99   100

Image of letter = verbal WM
Image of Mr X = visual–spatial WM
Scores that fall within the shaded category are in
the average range

Figure 4.1   Working memory profile of math difficulties

'4 × 6 = 24'. They then use their working memory like a mental black-board to work with these facts to solve problems they don't know, for example '(36 + 3)/ ? = 13'. But because of a poor working memory, a student with dyscalculia has a hard time compiling their math library, and working with the facts in their library at the same time.

Consider Robert, who struggles with mental math because numbers 'don't stay in my head'. Even when they are written down, he has a hard time solving the problem because he gets stuck at the simplest steps, for example recognizing number magnitude (such as 37 coming before 38). Robert has memorized very few math facts, so he doesn't have a foundation of knowledge that is readily available. Take the problem '37 + 6'. Robert doesn't know the math fact that '7 + 6 = 13', so he has to use his working memory to go up the number line from seven, by ones, six times. His work-ing memory has spent so much effort figuring the answer for the numbers in the ones place, that he forgets to add the 1 to the 3 (in the tens place), and writes down 33 as the answer instead. A typically developing student can use their working memory to retrieve basic math facts from their long-term memory and apply them to the problem. But because Robert has to use his working memory to solve the basic steps of the problem, he has to work twice as hard just to get an incorrect answer.

The math skills of students with dyscalculia appear behind what they should be for their age group. The National Center for Learning Disabilities in the USA has identified common math deficits for students with dyscalculia according to their age, and in the following section we will consider the possible role of working memory in these problems.

Working memory and dyscalculia in the early years

Younger children have trouble recognizing printed numbers and learning to count. Number recognition requires children to use their visual–spatial working memory to bind the visual information with the numerical concept. In other words, we need our working memory to associate the graphic symbol '1' with the number concept 'one'. Children with dyscalculia may confuse 2 with 8 or 6 with 9 because they have not mastered this association.

We also use working memory to move information into long-term memory so that we don't have to constantly relearn it when we need it. This is an efficient process that frees up working memory to accomplish a task. Children with dyscalculia struggle to count because their limited working memory makes it hard for them to transfer number knowledge to their long-term memory. As a consequence, counting doesn't become automatic and they have to relearn the number line, wasting valuable working memory resources.

Working memory and dyscalculia in middle childhood

As students with dyscalculia reach school age, the fact that they haven't memorized math facts is exacerbated by having to solve more complex math calculations that require working memory. Although they are becoming familiar with the number line and simple facts of magnitude for a small set of numbers, they are now expected to dramatically expand that knowledge, for example by becoming familiar with number progressions from 1 to 100 or 1000, rather than just 1 to 10. This lack of knowledge greatly taxes their working memory, leaving little room for processing even simple arithmetical functions. Eventually they learn these things to a degree; however, they are constantly 'behind' as they are expected to solve more complex math problems, like '$(15 + 23)n = 114$'. Their working memory gets stuck on adding the $15 + 23$ as this information is not automatized and they get lost in the multi-step process.

Word problems are also an issue for students with math difficulty because they have to use their working memory not only to read and understand the problem, but also to process and solve the math functions. The latter aspect can overload working memory if some of the math knowledge is not automatized. As in the multi-step problem described previously, students with dyscalculia can also get lost in the process of completing a word problem and end up giving up on the activity.

Working memory and dyscalculia in adulthood

By the time they reach adulthood, they may have built up a good-sized library of basic math facts; but they now struggle to use their working memory to understand more sophisticated math concepts, like finding a square root, which in order to solve successfully, synthesizes knowledge of more than one math function like multiplication and number magnitude.

Working memory in students with both math and reading difficulties

Psychologists estimate that 50% of students with dyscalculia also have reading disabilities. This group is often referred to as students with specific learning disorder, and they have deficits in both verbal and visual–spatial working memory. But do the working memory deficits in these students vary as a result of the severity of learning deficits? In other words, do those with mild learning difficulties have mild working memory problems, while those with severe learning difficulties have worse working memory scores? A study comparing the working memory scores of students with mild and severe learning difficulties found a clear pattern: working memory deficits corresponded with the learning difficulties. Those with mild learning difficulties only had mild working memory problems, while those with severe learning needs had worse working memory scores. The take-home message is that students with both math and reading difficulties often have very poor working memory and need additional support in the classroom (Alloway et al., 2005a).

HOW: Strategies to support working memory

Two types of strategies are discussed here: **general working memory strategies** that can be applied to students with general learning needs, and **specific working memory strategies** for students with dyscalculia. While the general strategies below are tailored for those with math difficulties, you can modify them as appropriate for other students in your classroom.

General strategies

Use visual representation to support working memory. Students with dyscalculia have poor visual–spatial working memory, particularly in tasks that involve numbers. Encourage them to develop visual strategies or cues like markers on a text or highlighting crucial information, to support their working memory. A British teacher describes how she supported Lucy, 12 years old, when she was teaching the algebraic concept of negative exponents. The teacher told Lucy that in order to solve the problem, she had to flip the numbers upside-down, so 3^{-2} is solved like this: $1/3^2$. However, despite the teacher spending a week explaining and modeling the steps, Lucy still couldn't seem to grasp the concept. The teacher was at a loss until she spotted pictures Lucy had drawn in the margins of her notebook. She remembered that Lucy loved art class and asked her to draw a picture of a man upside-down to remind her of what to do in order to solve negative exponents. You can see a reproduction of Lucy's drawing in Figure 4.2. The teacher encouraged Lucy to use drawings as a visual reminder to solve other algebraic problems.

Figure 4.2 Lucy's drawing

Reduce working memory processing in activities. Present math problems *vertically* rather than horizontally. We use working memory to count when solving single-digit problems and to maintain the operand and interim results in multi-digit problems. When sums are presented horizontally, it requires more working memory processing to keep the numbers in mind and carry the correct number to solve the problem. Students are far more likely to make errors when they have to keep each step of the procedure in mind. However, by presenting math problems *vertically*, you reduce the processing load and make it less effortful.

Use learning tools and visual aids to support working memory processing. Tools such as graph paper to help the student organize rows and columns for a math problem, and calculators in a multi-step problem, can reduce the working memory processing involved in a math activity.

Early years strategy. Unifix blocks (math counting blocks) are a useful method to solve a math problem without overloading their working memory. For example, when adding double-digit numbers, the student with math difficulties can use the counting cubes to visualize the problem, while using their working memory to solve the ones column first and then the tens column next.

Shorten activities to reduce the working memory load. Time is a key component in working memory performance, as time pressure can make a manageable task too demanding. If the student with working memory deficits does not have enough time to process the information, they can become frustrated. For example, if they have to complete 20 math problems in 10 minutes they are unlikely to attempt them. They may either act up in class to shift the focus away from their struggles with the activity or sit quietly at their desk to avoid detection.

Early years strategy. Another example of how activities can overload working memory is when homework is given out. In one classroom, homework was frequently given out in the last few minutes of a lesson when students were finishing their class work. Students with poor working memory couldn't cope with the demands of having to finish one task, listen to instructions about their homework, and write it in their planner. But when the teacher wrote down the homework assignment on the board every morning, the students had enough time to copy the information into their planner.

Specific strategies

Automatize math facts. Students with dyscalculia often struggle with math facts and so they have to use their working memory to remember them instead of solving a multi-digit math problem. One learning-support teacher describes how she worked with Graham, 12 years old, to learn his multiplication tables. She introduced a multi-sensory strategy of 'piano tables' where Graham tapped his fingers in sequence from left to right while reciting multiples of two (example: 2, 4, 6, etc.). He was then able to use his fingers to support his answers to questions, e.g., 5 × 2 by tapping five fingers and saying the number. Similarly, when asked how many 2s were in 16, he tapped his fingers till he reached the correct number. Repeated practice helped him develop greater fluency in recalling the multiples.

Model the use of memory aids. While many classrooms have wonderful visual aids for math like number lines, wall charts, and Unifix blocks, students with learning difficulties often fail to use them. Why don't they integrate these memory aids in their class work? Unfortunately, the student with dyscalculia finds it too overwhelming to cope with the multiple demands of remembering what the teacher said, processing that information, as well as finding a suitable memory aid to support their learning.

Early years strategy. Thus, it is important for the teacher to model and reinforce the use of these visual aids. Take a number line and encourage the students to count in ascending and descending order. When they are familiar with using these visual aids, you can integrate them with a math problem. This way, the students' working memory can be devoted to solving the math problem rather than figuring out how to use the visual aid.

Provide a sample math problem to support working memory. The combination of poor math automaticity and working memory deficits means that students with dyscalculia are not able to organize their thoughts and plan how to solve a math problem. One way to support working memory in math is to provide 'worked-out answers' so students can see the steps in solving the math problem.

Cooperative learning. Students with dyscalculia can work with a classmate to learn how to apply 'worked-out answers' to a new math problem. This cooperative approach to learning math is effective in reducing processing difficulties that are associated with math anxiety. Studies that have examined cooperative learning found that math reasoning skills improve and continue to develop up to a year later.

Case Study: James

James' behaviors in relation to the dyscalculia checklist by the National Center for Learning Disabilities were:

- Trouble learning math facts (addition, subtraction, multiplication, division)
- Difficulty developing math problem-solving skills
- Poor long-term memory for math functions
- Unfamiliarity with math vocabulary

(Continued)

(Continued)

James, 13 years old, was in the 8th grade. He was moved into my remedial math course because he was struggling in his regular math class, and barely made it through his last two years of mathematics. I began evaluating him by giving him a basic math worksheet with problems like '24 − 12' and '14 + 910'. He was not sure what '+' and '−' signs meant and, as a result, could not complete the problems. Even when I told him what the symbols represented, he struggled to solve the problem. When he eventually grasped what the math signs meant ('+' means addition, '−' means subtraction, etc.), he forgot them by the next class.

He also did not know the order of steps required to solve a multi-digit math problem. For instance, when given the problem '910 + 14', James guessed instead of working out the steps. Even when I prompted him to start adding the numbers in the ones place, followed by the tens place, and finally the hundreds' place, he could not follow the steps.

Even mental math proved to be difficult for James. I wrote single-digit math problems on the board (5 + 8) and students raised their hands when they knew the answer. James never raised his hand during these exercises. When I sat with him one-on-one and did this exercise with him after school one day in a tutoring session, he still struggled and was not able to come up with an answer.

Strategies

- Automatize math facts

The first week we worked on learning the terminology of math symbols. I gave James a set of flashcards with the following symbols on the front: +, −, ×, ÷, and √. On the back, the corresponding names: add, subtract, multiply, divide, and square root. We reviewed these for the entire 50-minute class. I also wrote problems on a whiteboard in front of him and asked him what symbol was being used and what it meant.

I started with one math symbol on the first day and selected a new math symbol for each day. On Friday, I gave him a quiz with just the math symbol and a worksheet and asked him to identify which function was being used in a given problem. For instance, in the problem '10 + 19' he had to identify that the plus sign indicated that it was an addition problem. He did not have to solve the problem, just understand the symbol. He performed very well on the assignment and only missed one or two problems.

- Use visual aids to support working memory when memorizing math facts

With single-digit addition problems, I started by using sticks as a visual aid. I gave James the problem '3 + 6' and asked him to get two piles of sticks, one for 3 and the other for 6. He then combined the two piles to create the answer, 9. After learning that, I asked him to use his fingers for a similar problem, by counting up from the largest number to the smallest. For instance, for the problem '23 + 6', he began at 23, then used his fingers to count 6 higher than 23. He eventually learned this concept of using a number larger than 10, like '23 + 12'.

- Use visual representation to support working memory

I posted a chart with the instructions for each step on his desk. He was allowed to use this assistance chart for a week. Then I took the chart down and tested him, giving him prompts as he went along, to encourage good counting habits. He received a perfect score.

- Provide a sample math problem to support working memory

For math problems using division and square roots, I provided a sample problem for James to follow. This freed up his working memory to learn the steps. He started with just solving the first step of the problem, using my problem as a guide. The next day he moved on to the next step, again using my sample problem. This continued until he completed each step of the problem. After a week of this, he then solved the first step of the problem without looking at my example. Eventually, he solved the whole math problem on his own.

Case Study: Samantha

Samantha's behaviors in relation to the dyscalculia checklist by the National Center for Learning Disabilities were:

- Difficulty measuring things
- Trouble organizing things in a logical way
- Trouble with mental math

(Continued)

(Continued)

Samantha was a 15-year-old student in my 9th grade culinary course. As part of the introductory curriculum, every student was required to understand the basic measurements relating to food and recipes. I normally take a few days to introduce the types of kitchen equipment, what each tool is used for, and what each measurement means. After the first week, I gave a quiz on kitchen appliances, measurements, and simple conversions (example: How many ounces are in a cup? A UK equivalent might be to convert ounces to grams). Although Samantha could identify the appliances, she failed the measurements and conversions sections of the test.

The normal procedure for a student who fails this portion of the test is to have them follow a recipe written in ounces and then convert it to cup measurements. Samantha also did a very poor job on this procedure, and her recipe did not turn out as expected.

I decided to let Samantha continue in the course and paired her with a more able cooking team. However, her team noted that she was not contributing, as she was unable to take measurements and add them together for a recipe.

Strategies

- Automatize math facts

I took out each measuring tool and explained their names, labeling them to help Samantha remember. For instance, I took a tablespoon measurement and put a label on it that said 'tablespoon'. Once she mastered these measurements, she was able to use the tools in her group to make recipes.

- Use visual representation to support working memory

I helped Samantha learn the conversions from ounces to cups, and teaspoons to tablespoons. I took a one-cup measuring tool and labeled it as 8 ounces. I kept repeating the measurement to her, and made her repeat it to me as well.

I also gave her a picture guide of the conversions to use as reference. After a month of teaching her the conversion rules, I quizzed her again and found that she had improved greatly, especially when questions included visual information.

- Model the use of visual aids

I then presented Samantha with complex questions like 'If 1 cup is 8 ounces, how many ounces is ½ cup?' I wrote out the problem and used two measuring cups, filling a 1-cup measurement to the top and the other 1-cup halfway. After Samantha watched me model this, she was able to understand that ½ cup is equivalent to 4 ounces. I allowed her to use the labeled tools for a few weeks until she was familiar with them.

Case Study: Christopher

Christopher's behaviors in relation to the dyscalculia checklist by the National Center for Learning Disabilities were:

- Difficulty estimating costs like grocery bills
- Difficulty learning math concepts beyond the basic math facts
- Poor ability to budget or balance a checkbook or account

Christopher was a 20-year-old adult who had just moved out of his parents' home. He worked as a phone customer service representative for a cell phone company. For the first time ever, Christopher was in charge of his own shopping and keeping track of his accounts, though his parents supported his living costs. His money from his job was supposed to cover his food and other daily expenses. However, after his first paycheck he was forced to dip into his savings to make ends meet.

His mother went to his house to discuss his banking and called me, a finance teacher, to work with Christopher on his budgeting. Part of my finance program requires Christopher to take me on a grocery-shopping trip with him. I asked him to buy five items that, without tax, would cost $20. After he collected his five items, I added them together and discovered that he had gathered $35 worth of items.

Strategies

- Reduce working memory processing in activities

I asked Christopher to find just two items that equalled $10. He did well on this task. I then asked for more items, increasing the total monetary value.

- Use learning tools to support working memory processing

Christopher used a calculator to add up his purchases as he added more items to his shopping cart. I then removed the use of a calculator and

(Continued)

(Continued)

asked Christopher to use a notebook to list every food purchase he made. After a four-week period, he tallied all his purchases and used this amount to create a weekly grocery budget. Each week, he used his grocery list in his notebook as a guide for purchases and he would add his purchases as he went along to make sure he stuck to his budget.

• Use learning tools to support working memory processing

I encouraged him to round up the dollar amounts and only add one item at a time. For instance, he would get his first item, worth $0.99 (rounded up to $1.00), and store that amount in his working memory. His next item cost $3.99 (rounded up to $4.00), and he would add that to his first price of $1.00. He followed these steps till he completed all his purchases.

At the end of the month, he was able to balance his checkbook and create a suitable budget so he did not overspend on items like groceries. When he balanced his budget properly, his reward was being able to save money and become more independent from his parents.

Summary

1. **Core deficit**: Students with math difficulties have poor number sense, which results in difficulties learning number rules and arithmetic facts in younger children, and solving complex arithmetic and word problems in older children.
2. **Working memory profile**: Students with math difficulties have impairments in *visual–spatial working memory*. Young students (5–7 years) can also have verbal working memory deficits, while older students (8 years and older) may have average verbal working memory.
3. **Strategies**: Support these students to automatize math facts and use visual representation to minimize working memory processing.

References and further reading

Alloway, T.P. and Passolunghi, M.C. (2011) The relations between working memory and arithmetical abilities: a comparison between Italian and British children. *Learning and Individual Differences*, 21: 133–7.

Alloway, T.P., Gathercole, S.E., Adams, A.M., Willis, C., Eaglen, R., and Lamont, E. (2005a) Working memory and other cognitive skills as predictors of progress towards early learning goals at school entry. *British Journal of Developmental Psychology*, 23: 417–26.

Alloway, T.P., Gathercole, S.E., Willis, C., and Adams, A.M. (2005b) Working memory and special educational needs. *Educational and Child Psychology*, 22: 56–67.

Bird, R. (2013) *The Dyscalculia Toolkit*, 2nd edn. London: Sage.

Bird, R. (2009) *Overcoming Difficulties with Number.* London: Sage.

Bugden, S., Price, G.R., McLean, D.A., and Ansari, D. (2012) The role of the left intraparietal sulcus in the relationship between symbolic number processing and children's arithmetic competence. *Developmental Cognitive Neuroscience*, 2: 448–57.

Friso-van den Bos, I., van der Ven, S., Kroesbergen, E., and van Luit, J. (2013) Working memory and mathematics in primary school children: a meta-analysis. *Educational Research Review*, 10: 29–44.

Geary, D. (2011) Cognitive predictors of achievement growth in mathematics: a 5-year longitudinal study. *Developmental Psychology*, 47: 1539–52.

Geary, D., Hoard, M.K., Nugent, L., and Bailey, D. (2012) Mathematical cognition deficits in children with learning disabilities and persistent low achievement: a five year prospective study. *Journal of Educational Psychology*, 104: 206–23.

Raghubar, K., Barnes, M., and Hecht, S. (2010) A review of developmental, individual difference, and cognitive approaches. *Learning and Individual Differences*, 20: 110–22.

Vicario, C.M., Rappo, G., Pepi, A., Pavan, A., and Martino, D. (2012) Temporal abnormalities in children with developmental dyscalculia. *Developmental Neuropsychology*, 37: 636–52.

CHAPTER 5

DEVELOPMENTAL COORDINATION DISORDER (DCD)

This chapter looks at:

- WHAT is developmental coordination disorder (DCD)?
- WHERE are the affected brain regions?
- WHY is working memory linked to DCD?
- HOW can working memory be supported in students with DCD?

Look at the writing sample in Figure 5.1. It was written by Tom, a 12-year-old with average IQ, diagnosed with developmental coordination disorder (DCD). Because he struggles with fine motor control, he has difficulties holding a pencil or pen correctly, mastering basic letter patterns, even writing at a normal speed. Here is what Tom said: 'I hate writing assignments! I know I am the slowest and always feel nervous. I wish I didn't have to do them.' In the classroom, fine-motor-skills deficits manifest themselves most obviously in writing.

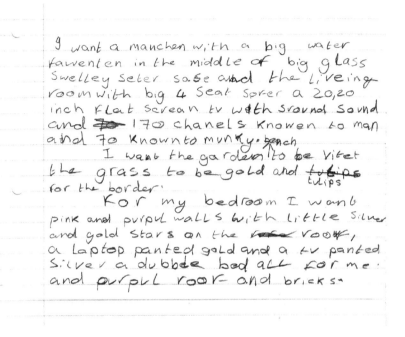

Figure 5.1 Sample writing

Try It: Fine motor skills

Here is an exercise to test your motor skills. Hold a pencil in your non-dominant hand; so if you normally write with your right hand, then hold a pencil in your left hand. How did you feel holding the pencil? Did it take some time to find a comfortable position? Did you readjust your pencil position often?

Now write a sentence and ask someone to read it. Will they find it difficult to decipher what you have written? How does this writing compare with your normal writing? You have just experienced some of the motor coordination problems that a student with DCD goes through.

WHAT it is

Writing is not the only difficulty that students with DCD experience. DCD is characterized by a wide range of both motor and visual difficulties.

Picture this scene: Susie runs over to meet her friends in the playground; she trips over her feet, but picks herself up and laughs it off. While her friends are scrambling from side to side on the climbing frame, Susie sticks to the slide. She knows if she goes slowly, she won't trip on the ladder. She hates PE. She is always the last to get picked for teams and usually gets so nervous that she can't catch the ball or drops it when she does occasionally catch it. To avoid going to PE, Susie always volunteers to help the teacher organize materials in the classroom. Sometimes she gets mixed up when the teacher tells her to put things away, but she prefers that to PE.

You may recognize a student like Susie in your class. They struggle with their balance, have trouble distinguishing left from right, lack spatial awareness, and experience low self-esteem as a result of these difficulties. Young children find it difficult to pick up math counters, to do up their coat buttons before going outside, and to tie their shoelaces. Older children find it difficult to use a keyboard as a result of their poor motor skills, even though using it can alleviate their problems with writing.

Visual deficits are also linked with movement control and motor learning. For example, students with DCD have poor tracking skills, which means that they may not notice an oncoming ball until it is too late to catch it. Nor can they judge the speed or distance of an oncoming vehicle. Three-dimensional vision is poor and so they often misjudge the distance of chairs and tables and have difficulty finding objects on patterned surfaces.

DSM and diagnosis

Classifications such as minimal brain dysfunction, perceptual-motor dysfunction, physical awkwardness, and clumsiness have all been used to describe individuals with motor difficulties. DCD is usually diagnosed by a health professional, such as a pediatrician or an occupational therapist. Diagnosis is based on performance on standardized tests, such as the Movement Assessment Battery for Children (MABC-2) or the Bruininks–Oseretsky Test of Motor Proficiency.

Clinical observations are based on *DSM-5* and include the following:

- Poor motor skills compared to their same-age peers
- Motor impairments negatively impact daily activities
- No other medical condition such as cerebral palsy

There are also screening tools available for educators to use. While these are not meant for diagnosis, they provide the teacher with useful information regarding the student's motor skills. The Movement ABC (M-ABC), an observational checklist for teachers, provides a descriptive account of motor skills in daily activities.

WHERE it is: Working memory and the DCD brain

Because DCD has a wide range of motor and visual symptoms, it is difficult to identify the brain regions responsible for DCD behavior and how they interact with working memory. Only one study so far has looked at brain activity when children with DCD are performing a visual–spatial working memory task. Children were shown pictures of ladybirds on grids and asked to compare their positions. Not only did the children with DCD take longer to give their answer; they also performed worse than typically developing children and also had very different brain patterns. The children with DCD showed smaller processing capacity in the prefrontal cortex, the home of working memory, suggesting that their working memory was weaker than their peers when making spatial comparisons (Tsai et al., 2012).

WHY working memory is linked to DCD

Case Study: Joshua

'Tonight I read an article on your research findings regarding poor memory. I was immediately drawn to the article as my son Joshua is struggling at school and receives extra help from the school's SENCO [special educational needs coordinator] – the school are very supportive. She feels he exhibits dyspraxic (DCD) tendencies but we also both feel that his biggest barrier to learning is his poor working memory. This affects all areas of his learning. His long-term memory for places visited, people he has met, is fantastic yet he can get no further than the first line of nursery rhymes he has heard since birth. He tries so hard but learning spelling [words] and acting on instructions is a real struggle for him.'

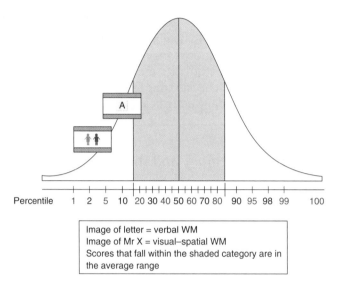

Percentile   1   2   5   10   20 30 40 50 60 70 80   90 95 98 99   100

> Image of letter = verbal WM
> Image of Mr X = visual–spatial WM
> Scores that fall within the shaded category are in
> the average range

Figure 5.2   Working memory profile of DCD

A poor visual–spatial working memory is the primary working memory weakness in students with DCD. When compared to their peers who don't have DCD, they are seven times more likely to achieve lower scores in visual–spatial working memory. As Figure 5.2 shows, their working memory is well below what is expected for their age. Why do they find tasks that involve visual–spatial working memory, like copying a list from a board and keeping track of their place, so difficult? Studies confirm that we use our visual–spatial working memory to plan and control our movements. When it is impaired, we struggle with tasks involving spatial planning.

Have you ever tried to tap your head and rub your stomach at the same time? It's not easy to do the first time, but you can get used to it. This task is forcing you to do two different motor movements at the same time, and in order to successfully do it, you have to use your working memory. Now add another task, tapping out the rhythm to 'Happy Birthday' with your foot, while making sure that you aren't matching that rhythm with the hand tapping your head. This third addition with your foot may overload your working memory, causing you to become muddled. A student with DCD faces a similar challenge every time they have to use their visual–spatial working memory, like when they are copying a list from the board, and have to keep track of their place in a written activity.

Working memory and DCD in the early years

Fine-motor-skills difficulty impacts handwriting in young children. In written work, they have the combined difficulty of struggling to hold their pencil while recruiting an underperforming working memory to assist them in completing a classroom activity. As a result, even simple tasks like copying a sentence from the board can prove overwhelming for them.

Working memory and DCD in middle childhood

Because visual–spatial working memory is so important for classroom success, students with DCD often experience poor learning outcomes. This was confirmed by comparing the academic performance of two groups of students with DCD: one with very poor visual–spatial working memory skills and another with comparatively high visual–spatial working memory skills. The low visual–spatial working memory group performed much worse than those with high visual–spatial working memory in standardized tests of reading and math. In other words, their working memory determined their grades.

IQ, working memory, and DCD. We know that IQ is linked to learning for typically developing students. Students with DCD usually score very low on nonverbal IQ tests, especially in tests involving a motor component such as moving blocks around (example: Block Design and Object Assembly subtests from the WISC). In a study to find out if working memory is more important than IQ in determining grades in students with DCD (Alloway, 2007), students' IQ and working memory were measured and a statistical procedure used to equate IQ levels across both groups. Now it was possible to compare their working memory to find out whether those with low visual–spatial working memory would still get lower grades than their higher visual–spatial working memory counterparts. A similar pattern emerged: poor working memory resulted in poor grades in students with DCD.

DCD and learning disabilities. Working memory seems to be a key player in academic success or failure. However, does the poor working memory in students with DCD result in worse academic performance compared to students with learning disabilities with a stronger working memory? Alloway and Temple (2007) found that when students with DCD have worse working memory scores than those with learning disabilities, they have worse grades as a result.

DCD and specific language impairment (SLI). Additional support for this finding came when students with DCD were compared with those with specific language impairment (SLI; Alloway and Archibald, 2008). SLI is a disorder characterized by poor language skills but average IQ. Students with SLI often have a hard time forming words in the past tense, and have a smaller vocabulary than typically developing students. Students with SLI also have a stronger working memory than those with DCD. Comparing their grades revealed yet again that the poor working memory of the DCD students resulted in worse grades. The poor working memory of a student with DCD is driving their academic struggles. The converse may also be true: by supporting their poor working memory, we can improve their grades.

Current Debate: Sensory processing disorder – what makes a disorder?

Did you ever play Marco Polo as a child? I used to love closing my eyes and spinning around faster and faster when I was 'It'. Now imagine playing that game in the middle of a busy traffic intersection. Cars are honking, dogs are barking, siren sounds get closer, and people are yelling. You are 'It' and are trying to listen to where the 'Polo' is coming from. For a student who is hypersensitive to sound, touch, and light, the world is a chaotic place. As a result, new surroundings can be very disorienting for them. This difficulty is often referred to as sensory processing disorder (SPD), also known as sensory integration dysfunction.

This label may come as a welcome relief to some parents, who want an explanation for why their child has not reached certain developmental milestones, like walking or talking. Yet, does a label like SPD actually benefit parents? There are many psychologists who think that the label of SPD is actually doing parents a disservice. There are several reasons why this is the case. The first is that the difficulties associated with SPD reflect a neurodevelopmental immaturity, which means that the child will likely outgrow the symptoms naturally without the need for expensive and unproven treatments. Although it is a condition identified by some health practitioners, it is not recognized as a disorder in *DSM-5*.

The next issue is that the features of SPD are often symptomatic of more serious disorders such as DCD, ADHD, and ASD. Thus, a label of SPD might falsely lead a parent to feel comforted that their child is receiving support, when more serious problems might be going undiagnosed, and as a result, untreated.

Finally, there are very few published clinical trials on either the diagnosis of SPD or the treatment of it. Those that are published have been criticized as flawed research, due to small sample sizes. It appears then that while the symptoms of SPD are real, they point to more serious disorders that merit an accurate diagnosis and appropriate treatment.

Working memory and DCD in adulthood

For adults with DCD, learning new tasks that involve motor skills is particularly difficult, such as learning to drive or familiarizing themselves with the motor demands of a new task. One study that interviewed adults with DCD reported that they found parallel parking or driving in reverse particularly difficult and that 'just getting the feel of driving a car was not very easy'. Combine this motor difficulty with the working memory burden of navigating the roads, judging traffic conditions, and anticipating other drivers' movements as you maneuver a busy highway. Juggling all this information can overburden any skilled driver, and it is easy to see how an adult with DCD may prefer to avoid driving during busy periods, or even altogether.

The workplace can pose similar difficulties for an adult with DCD, particularly if they are starting a new job. Their working memory has to focus on learning the ropes, but their motor difficulties mean that their working memory has to be diverted to support learning new motor skills, resulting in frustration and disappointment when they are not able to live up to expectations. One adult with DCD described his experiences as a result of an overloaded working memory in the workplace: 'I've worked lots of different factory jobs. Probably the worst one was I worked in a muffler factory with welding machines. I have burns all over my arms from that place' (Missiuna et al., 2008).

HOW: Strategies to support working memory

In this section, we present **general working memory strategies** tailored for students with DCD. You can also modify them as appropriate for other students in your classroom.

Use visual representation to support working memory

The student with DCD has poor visual–spatial working memory so it is important to support the learning activity or the task with visual prompts.

With older students with DCD, their poor working memory may result in forgetting to bring the right textbook to the right class. You can place the class schedule directly on the student's desk and even include a photo of the textbooks on the schedule so the student can match up the right textbook with the right class.

One teacher pointed out that her classroom has a magic whiteboard in the front of the class and students will go up to refer to it and touch it to find out the next lesson. As with many classroom visual aids, many students benefit from it. But the student with DCD may get confused with having to walk up to the board and point to the correct place on the schedule and then go back to their desk to get the right book. For these students, the key is to make these visual prompts directly accessible to them. Include an arrow on the class schedule on the student's desk so they can move it to remind themselves of their place on the schedule.

This will allow them to use their working memory to focus on the lesson instead of trying to figure out what book they need.

Early years strategy. A teacher from Florida shared this tip. Every time she asked the class to go to get their lunchbox and stand by the door, Carrie, 6 years old, would wander aimlessly around the classroom while the rest of the students were ready to go. The teacher had spent time making this instruction a part of their daily routine so the students knew exactly where to go to get their lunchboxes and what to do next. She regularly repeated the information step by step, yet Carrie still needed constant prompting. Her solution was to give Carrie a photo of her lunchbox and also stick the same photo on her cubbyhole at the back of the class. The photo helped Carrie stay on track so she knew what she had to do and where to go. It wasn't long before Carrie was so fast that she was first in line after getting her lunchbox!

Reduce working memory processing in activities

Writing is another activity that is extremely effortful for the student with DCD. Their difficulty is two-fold: their motor difficulties mean that they struggle to form letters, while their poor visual–spatial working memory impacts their ability to keep a thread of ideas when writing. They spend so much effort trying to form the letters correctly that they run out of working memory 'space' and forget what they wanted to write. The result is a disjointed and hard-to-read paragraph. To circumvent this problem, try letting the student use speech-to-text software for some writing activities. This will allow them to focus on communicating their ideas rather than on the mechanics of writing.

Early years strategy. Assigning a buddy or student helper is another great way to reduce working memory processing in classroom activities, especially for younger children. Often the student with DCD takes longer to complete physical tasks, like tidying their desk and putting away materials. They can work in pairs to complete these daily tasks quickly and keep up with the rest of the class. To avoid them feeling like 'the odd one out' if they are the only ones working with a buddy, pair up other students too.

Minimize distractions so working memory is not overwhelmed

Classrooms walls are often plastered with posters of the alphabet, multiplication tables, animals under the sea, and so on. For many students these are wonderful visual prompts to support the information they are learning. However, for the student with poor visual–spatial working memory, the process of looking around to find the relevant information and then match it to their work at their desk is too effortful. As a result, they often lose their place in the activity or abandon doing it altogether. Prevent this working memory overload by seating them next to a blank wall or uncluttered space. This will allow them to direct their working memory to focus on the task.

Current Debate: Can exercise improve learning?

In the last few years, there have been various claims in the media on how simple exercises like jumping jacks and balancing can make children smarter. So is there any basis to these claims? Let's first look at the evidence for whether exercise improves motor skills. If the exercise is simple, like skipping, then you notice improvement in skipping skills very quickly. However, if the exercise is relatively complicated, like hockey-puck shooting, then there is very little improvement, even after over 1000 practices!

What about learning? Tracy recruited students with DCD to take part in a 13-week exercise program (Alloway and Warner, 2008). One-half of the group did different balancing exercises, as well as Brain Gym-type activities. The other half of the group did not participate in any of these physical activities. They were called the control group: we could measure the progress of the exercise group against the control group.

At the end of the 13 weeks, the students in the exercise group had better motor skills compared to the control group. But there was no impact on their grades. Their reading and math scores were still very low.

What does this study mean? While exercise is great for the brain and the body, this study, and a growing number like this, illustrate that it's not enough to ask students to do some jumping jacks and skipping if we actually want to help them do better in the classroom. We need to address the foundation of learning – working memory – to see improvements in grades as well.

Case Study: Robert – fine motor difficulties

Robert's behaviors in relation to *DSM-5*:

- Performance in daily activities that require motor coordination is substantially below that expected
- Poor handwriting

(Continued)

(Continued)

Robert, 7 years old, was struggling in his 1st grade class. His issues weren't noticeable until we started using pencils in class. Part of the curriculum for writing requires the student to write and repeat what he has written. Robert struggled with grasping the pencil. When he finally wrote something, it was not within the specified lines on the paper.

This year was the first year that Robert began creative writing, based on a topic of his choice. Robert told me he was very interested in writing about his grandmother. However, when he had to work independently to begin writing, he just sat there staring at his paper. When I walked over to him and to ask how his writing was going, I noticed that there was nothing on the paper but line drawings.

Strategies

- Reduce working memory processing by supporting fine motor skills

To start the activity, I asked Robert to write his name on the top of the paper. He struggled to hold the pencil in his hand. I took a rubber band out of my desk and used it to attach the pencil to his palm in the proper position. He was then able to write his name with relative ease.

- Keep track of his place in complex activities

When the class listened to a book on tape, Robert used a popsicle stick to follow along with the narrator in his book. This freed up his working memory to understand the text rather than keep up with the reading.

- Break down information to reduce working memory processing

I sat with Robert and discussed the topic that he wanted to write. I worked one-on-one with him until he could produce a good topic sentence and supporting sentences for his essay.

- Use visual representation to support working memory

I taught Robert how to create an outline using a spider diagram. In the center of the web I put the word 'grandmother' in a bubble and asked him what activities his grandmother did with him. He told me about a time his grandmother took him bowling, so I instructed him to draw a line from the bubble that 'grandmother' was written in, to a new bubble where he could write 'bowling'.

After he came up with three ideas I asked him to expand on each idea. For bowling, he created a new bubble that had the winner of the game within it. After doing this for each idea, I asked him to begin writing, first explaining who grandmother is, then talking about all of the topics that he had outlined.

- Shorten study periods or activities to reduce the working memory load

After every two sentences of writing, we stopped and took a 2-minute break where Robert read what he had written up till that point. The following week, he wrote an additional sentence before taking a break. Eventually he was able to write a paragraph in one sitting before he needed to take a break.

Case Study: Tammy – gross motor difficulties

Tammy's behaviors in relation to *DSM-5*:

- Performance in daily activities that require motor coordination is substantially below that expected
- Dropping things
- Clumsiness
- Poor performance in sports

Tammy, 11 years old, was in my 5th grade class. At first, she seemed like a normal young girl, albeit slightly clumsy and uncoordinated. However, as time progressed I noticed a few areas of concern. On the first day of class, she ran into my desk and scattered a stack of papers onto the floor. I asked her to help me pick them up and she began what seemed like a lazy attempt. She was grabbing at papers, not grasping them completely, and seemed to have great difficulty picking them up off the floor. Since this was the first time she had done this, I didn't think it was an issue.

  As time progressed, Tammy's motor difficulties were becoming a problem in the classroom. One day she was sitting at her desk when I heard a huge crash. I looked over to her and noticed she was on the ground next to her desk. When I rushed over to her and asked her what happened, she simply said 'I fell'. She slouched in her chair so it occurred to me that her poor posture probably led to her falling out of her chair. I then began receiving reports from her physical education teacher that she was struggling in team sports and constantly ended up in the nurse's clinic with bumps and bruises.

(Continued)

(Continued)

Tammy also has issues with following directions. When I escorted the class to their elective class for the day, I gave them left and right directions. When it was her turn to lead the class, she mixed up her right and left and often ended up at the wrong class.

Strategies

- Reduce working memory processing by supporting gross motor skill

After I started noticing Tammy's motor difficulties, I began supporting her more in class. If she began to slouch, I encouraged her to correct her posture. When she was walking in class, I kept my eye on her and if she began to veer, I called out her name and she would correct herself. This reduced her incidences of knocking things over and hurting herself.

- Use visual representation to support working memory

I took strips of colored tape and laid them in lines around the classroom to guide Tammy's movements. If she needed to get from A to B, she just had to follow a line. I instructed her to keep the line between her legs as she walked. This controlled her bumping into desks and tables as well.

I also taught Tammy a trick to tell directions. Take both hands and put them in front of your face. Raise just the thumb and pointer finger. Your left hand will make the shape of an 'L' as in 'Left'. As I called out the direction the class needed to turn, Tammy raised her hands in front of her and used that trick to see which direction was left. I also suggested that she hold up her writing hand to remember which direction was right (she was right-handed).

Case Study: Tad – fine and gross motor difficulties

Tad's behaviors in relation to *DSM-5*:

- Performance in daily activities that require motor coordination is substantially below that expected
- Poor handwriting

Tad, 20 years old, was a junior at a state university. I worked as a tutor at the university's student center. Tad's biggest issue was his writing ability. He had such bad handwriting that he could not even read his own notes. Neither could I. His classes did not allow the use of computers so he had to rely solely on his handwriting for his lecture notes. Since his notes were so poorly written, I asked him to start bringing his book to the tutoring center so we could go through it together.

Strategies

- Minimize distractions so working memory is not overwhelmed

The first thing I did was to move away from the busy tutoring center to the more quiet study rooms in the library. This meant that I had his full attention without distractions from others around us.

- Reduce working memory processing by supporting fine motor skills

We addressed Tad's handwriting skills by focusing on each letter individually. I asked him to write the alphabet repeatedly, making sure to focus on each letter to make sure it was legible. He would slowly copy a sentence so he could focus on each individual letter as he was writing. He did this repeatedly, progressively speeding up his writing time.

- Shorten study periods or activities to reduce the working memory load

Throughout our 2-hour study sessions, I would take short breaks with Tad every 20 minutes. In our 2- to 5-minute breaks we would watch a music video or just talk about his day. These breaks improved his overall progression, as he was able to produce tidy work immediately after a break. As Tad became better at writing and taking notes, I would allow for more break time in our sessions. If he did especially well and was able to produce legible notes from his class, I would end our tutoring sessions early.

- Reduce working memory processing by supporting gross motor skill

I was concerned about Tad's posture and I believed it was part of the reason his writing was so thick and illegible. I recommended he bring a small pillow to support his lower back (lumbar support). I instructed him to lean against the pillow and focus on maintaining a straight back as he wrote. His writing became lighter and more legible.

When Tad began showing improvements in his handwriting abilities, he also began getting better grades. This was the greatest motivation for him to continue working on his motor difficulties. When he focused on his posture and writing, he became a better student and it was reflected in his grades.

Summary

1. **Core deficit**: Students with DCD have difficulties with fine and gross motor skills, as well as visual problems.
2. **Working memory profile**: These students have impairments in visual–spatial working memory; Students with DCD are seven times more likely to have poor visual–spatial working memory compared to typically developing peers.
3. **Strategies**: Support these students by giving shorter instructions and activities; and reduce visual–spatial working memory processing in classroom activities.

References and further reading

Alloway, T.P. (2007) Working memory, reading and mathematical skills in children with developmental coordination disorder. *Journal of Experimental Child Psychology*, 96: 20–36.

Alloway, T.P. and Archibald, L.M. (2008) Working memory and learning in children with developmental coordination disorder and specific language impairment. *Journal of Learning Disabilities*, 41: 251–62.

Alloway, T.P. and Temple, K.J. (2007) A comparison of working memory profiles and learning in children with developmental coordination disorder and moderate learning difficulties. *Applied Cognitive Psychology*, 21: 473–87.

Alloway, T.P. and Warner, C. (2008) The effect of task-specific training on learning and memory in children with developmental coordination disorder. *Perceptual and Motor Skills*, 107: 273–80.

Henderson, S.E. and Sugden, D.A. (2007) *Movement ABC Checklist*. Harlow: Pearson Education.

Missiuna, C., Moll, S., King, G., Stewart, D., and MacDonald, K. (2008) Life experiences of young adults who have coordination difficulties. *Canadian Journal of Occupational Therapy*, 75: 157–66.

Tsai, C.L., Chang, Y.K., Hung, T.M., Tseng, Y.T., and Chen, T.C. (2012) The neurophysiological performance of visuospatial working memory in children with developmental coordination disorder. *Developmental Medicine & Child Neurology*, 54: 1114–20.

CHAPTER 6

ATTENTION DEFICIT/ HYPERACTIVITY DISORDER (ADHD)

This chapter looks at:

- WHAT is ADHD?
- WHERE are the affected brain regions?
- WHY is working memory linked to ADHD?
- HOW can working memory be supported in students with ADHD?

Jeremy is in a bad mood. He just fought with his mother on the way to school and now someone has taken the ball on the playground. He runs over and demands that they give it to him. But he can't wait so he pushes them and grabs the ball. He is sent to the principal's office. When asked why he acted that way, he says, 'I don't like being different. Everyone knows I am. I have a good side and a bad side in my brain and the bad side wins a lot. I can't help it, I just go bad like The Hulk and start pushing things over.'

The Hulk also surfaces in the classroom, according to his teacher. Jeremy has trouble sitting still, struggles to complete tasks on time, and is easily distracted. His working memory difficulties make it hard for him to keep track of what he needs to do, and he has a hard time reading information on the board. He is one of the first students to hand in his work but it is always full of errors, and sometimes is not even complete.

WHAT it is

Jeremy is one of the approximately 11% of children who are diagnosed with attention deficit/hyperactivity disorder (ADHD), one of the most commonly diagnosed behavioral disorders in children and young people (CDC, 2013). ADHD is composed of both **hyperactive/impulsive** behaviors (include fidgeting or talking excessively, difficulty in waiting one's turn, and frequently interrupting others) and **inattentive** behaviors (such as making careless mistakes in school, forgetfulness in daily activities, and being easily distracted). Students with ADHD are usually seen as having great difficulty remaining seated when required, and are much more active than their peers. They also find it hard to remember complex instructions, show poor attention to instructions, and find it hard not to interrupt with their comments.

Poor inhibition is a central feature in those with ADHD. Inhibition is the ability to control inappropriate behavior, thoughts, and speech. Inhibition is closely related to a cognitive skill called executive function, which helps plan, manage, and control behavior. Students with poor inhibition often do or think about the wrong things at the wrong time. For example, they may get up and walk around during a spelling test, or instead of writing down a sentence with the word 'dinosaur' in it, like they were asked to do, begin thinking about a cartoon they saw at home that featured a funny looking T-rex. A student who is hyperactive or impulsive is unlikely to learn effectively and often disrupts others.

Try It: Inhibition

Say these words as fast as you can:

Sun   Moon   Moon   Sun   Moon   Sun   Sun   Moon   Sun   Moon

Now say them as you see the pictures:

Now, here is the tricky part: say the opposite word of what you see. If the word is 'Sun', say 'MOON'; if the word is 'Moon', say 'SUN'.

Sun   Moon   Moon   Sun   Moon   Sun   Sun   Moon   Sun   Moon

How did you do? Here's a final one: say the opposite word of the picture you see:

It is a lot harder than it looks, isn't it? You had to inhibit or suppress your automatic response to say the word rather than its opposite. You may be familiar with a more common version where you have to say the color of a word rather than read the word, known as the Stroop test. This classic test of inhibition requires the individual to suppress an automatized skill – reading – in order to say the color of the word instead.

Students with ADHD also have difficulty in a related executive function skill that requires them to focus their attention on a single task – **sustained attention**. A common way to measure this is using a computer-based test where students see numbers flash on a screen. They have to click on the spacebar every time they see the number '5'. Students with ADHD are faster, but make more errors than their peers who do not have attention problems. If you watch them do the test, you will notice that they just press the spacebar for every number, rather than looking for just the number '5'. This is common in the classroom as well, as they have trouble monitoring their actions and so lose sight of the objective of the task.

If you have ever tried to get some grading or planning done when you have given your class an assignment to do, you may have a little sense of what ADHD can be like. You are trying to stay focused on your task, but you are constantly interrupted by students asking you questions, making it much harder for you to complete what you are trying to do. In much the same way that the interruptions you experience make it harder to finish, a student with ADHD struggles to inhibit inappropriate thoughts unrelated to their task, having a negative knock-on effect for the task they are trying to complete.

DSM and diagnosis

How can you tell whether a student like Jeremy has ADHD? Classroom behavior of students with ADHD is characterized by hyperactivity, inattention, and impulsiveness. However, the distinguishing feature between a student with ADHD and an energetic one is the degree and frequency of these features. The ADHD assessment considers biological, psychological, and social factors because students with ADHD usually show significant social, academic, and psychological difficulties at each stage of their development.

The DSM-5 criteria include:

- Eighteen symptoms related to inattention (example: easily distracted) and hyperactive/impulsive behavior (example: talks excessively)
- Individual must exhibit at least six symptoms to receive an ADHD diagnosis
- The onset age of symptoms has been changed from age 7 to age 12

While a diagnosis of ADHD typically involves a clinical interview, teachers can use a behavioral rating scale as an early screener of attention problems. Commonly used standardized teacher rating scales of classroom behavior include the Conners' Teacher Rating Scale (CTRS). [1]

WHERE it is: Working memory and the ADHD brain

A number of studies have investigated how the brain influences ADHD. Students with ADHD often have an underactive prefrontal cortex (PFC), the home of working memory. When students without ADHD get an urge to get up and walk around, or let their thoughts wander off to a television show they like, their working memory takes over, and helps them suppress the urge. But the working memory of a student with ADHD often isn't strong enough to exert control. This may be because students with ADHD often have a reduction in brain volume in the PFC.

At the same time, the motor cortex, which is responsible for planning and controlling motor functions, is overly active. This is like having a big, powerful engine under the hood of a car, constantly revving and trying to race around. The motor cortex is like the engine and the PFC (working memory) is the brake. If the brake isn't working that well, the result can be a behavior meltdown.

WHY working memory is linked to ADHD

In this section we discuss how poor working memory affects students with ADHD after age 12, in accordance with the *DSM-5* criteria. *DSM-5* recognizes that while students younger than 12 may display attentional and behavior problems, evidence shows that many of them will outgrow these patterns by the time they are 12.

It is also important to recognize that while some features of ADHD (like inattentive behaviors) and poor working memory are closely related, they are also distinct problems. While students with ADHD have a poor working memory, not all students with a poor working memory have ADHD. On the one hand, boys are four times more likely than girls to be diagnosed with ADHD, possibly because they act out their impulses, whereas girls internalize them by daydreaming instead. On the other hand, research on more than 3000 children demonstrated that boys are not more likely to have working memory problems compared to girls (Alloway et al., 2009a).

In addition to the characteristic hyperactive and impulsive behavior, students with ADHD also exhibit classroom behavior typical of working memory problems. Teachers report that these students have short attention spans and are easily distracted. They often forget what they are currently doing and things they have learned, fail to remember instructions, and leave

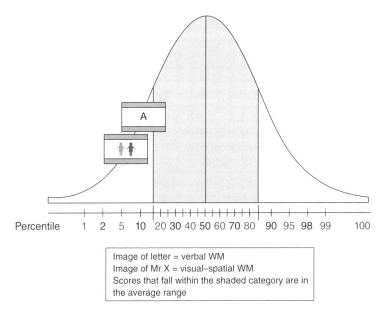

Figure 6.1 Working memory profile of ADHD

work incomplete. Because of their poor working memory, they find it effortful to process classroom information and, as a result, often make careless mistakes, particularly in writing, and have difficulty in solving problems.

Students with ADHD struggle when they have to process information. This deficit is evident when they are asked to remember lengthy instructions, keep track of their place in multi-step problems, or undertake activities that require multi-tasking. They will frequently complete only the first part of the instruction, lose track of where they are in the problem, or only complete one of the required activities.

Visual–spatial working memory deficits are also evident in the individual with ADHD. In fact, these deficits are so pervasive that a student with ADHD can be distinguished from students without ADHD by their low visual–spatial working memory scores. In one study, students with ADHD were given a range of executive function tests, such as inhibition, shifting, and planning actions, as well as working memory, to see which of these tests could best identify students with ADHD from their typically developing peers. Out of all the tests, visual–spatial working memory scores were the most accurate in identifying a student with ADHD in the classroom (Holmes et al., 2010). This tells us that visual–spatial working memory deficits are such a prominent feature of students with ADHD that they can be used as an additional tool to identify them in the classroom.

Working memory and inattention

A student with working memory problems is not necessarily hyperactive or impulsive. In fact, his or her behavior is very different. Take Michael for example. Michael has trouble remembering things, from what he is supposed to do next in an activity to what book he needs for a lesson. The teacher is often exasperated with him, but thinks that he is just a daydreamer. The truth is, Michael doesn't really cause problems in the classroom. He isn't boisterous or noisy. He doesn't even disturb his classmates. Just the opposite! He is usually sitting quietly at his desk. Often, he is doodling or staring out the window. But he is not doing the assignment. He has forgotten what to do and is too embarrassed to ask for help. Or he probably thinks: 'Why should I bother trying? I'm just going to get it wrong anyway.'

Students like Michael fall below the teacher's radar. They aren't disrupting the class or bouncing off the walls, so the teacher doesn't notice there is a problem. Often problems are not picked up until it's too late and the student starts failing because they haven't grasped key concepts in the lesson or can't understand what to do and how to do it. One study of almost 1000 students (55% boys) found that students, like Michael, who are identified by their teachers as having poor attention were also flagged up as requiring additional educational support in the classroom (Alloway, Elliott, and Holmes, 2010). If we want to support such students, we need to spot early warning signs. We need to realize that these students aren't just daydreamers and they will continue to struggle for their whole academic career if they are not adequately supported.

However, these students show fewer symptoms and are more difficult to identify. How can educators spot such students in the classroom? One option is to directly measure working memory behaviors, as students with ADHD show a lot of the symptoms of a working memory impairment. A study based on teacher ratings using the Working Memory Rating Scale (see Chapter 2) found that students with ADHD displayed classroom behavior associated with poor working memory, such as raising their hand but forgetting their response, losing their place in a multi-step activity, and difficulty remaining on task (Alloway et al., 2009b).

Working memory and giftedness

Gifted students have abilities that exceed those of their typical peers. They learn faster, are inquisitive, curious, and are able to quickly understand complex concepts. However, some gifted students have behavioral problems that correspond with ADHD, so much so that they are diagnosed with the disorder. To find out how this was possible, Tracy worked together with the (US) National Association of Gifted Children to compare the behavior patterns of those with ADHD and gifted children. The gifted children displayed behavior problems consistent with ADHD, such as problems with authority, being highly distractible, and lacking motivation. Here is a case study of a boy from that research collaboration.

Case Study: Joseph

Joseph, 13 years old, was very articulate, and the testing session with him took longer than usual as he asked a lot of questions and initiated many discussions. His mother says that he spends hours and hours researching topics that he finds interesting, often not related to school. Despite these characteristics of giftedness, teacher ratings using the Conners' Rating Scale indicated a behavior consistent with ADHD. When asked about his motivation levels, his mother said that he was apathetic and negative about his school.

Some children, like Joseph, although gifted, are also diagnosed with ADHD. We call these children 'twice-exceptional' – meaning they are intellectually gifted, but have also been formally diagnosed with a learning difficulty like ADHD because of their behavior. Not all researchers agree that gifted children manifest behavioral problems *per se*, suggesting instead that the curriculum is not tailored to their needs, and many bright students are not being taught at the appropriate level.

Our research showed that the gifted students displayed similar oppositional and hyperactive behaviors compared to students with ADHD. Interestingly, both groups also had very similar IQ scores. Yet they had very different learning outcomes. Why? Looking more closely at their working memory scores revealed that their working memory profiles were very different. As you would expect, the gifted students had excellent working memory, which was linked to their above-average academic outcomes. In contrast, the ADHD students' poor working memory was linked to low achievement (Alloway and Elsworth, 2012; Alloway et al., 2014).

It was interesting to see that the negative behavior patterns in gifted students did not negatively impact their working memory performance or their academic outcomes. In contrast to students with ADHD, the oppositional and hyperactive behavior patterns in gifted children may instead stem from frustrations in the classroom: when environmental stimuli decrease, hyperactivity increases as a means of self-stimulation to compensate for the lack of cognitive stimulation. In other words, their abilities exceed the cognitive demands placed on them, and they misbehave because they are bored.

One key frustration is that the curriculum is not tailored to their needs, and many bright students are not being taught at their instructional level. Additionally, much of the regular curriculum is redundant for gifted students as they do not require the usual amount of repetition to master many skills. For example, researchers found that when as much as 60% of the curriculum was eliminated, gifted students equalled or even exceeded the achievement levels of matched students who were required to complete the regular curriculum (Reiss et al., 1993). In your own classroom, this means that a student who misbehaves, but also achieves good grades, may just need extra stimulation to improve their behavior, rather than a time-out.

Working memory and ADHD in adults

ADHD is a persistent deficit, and is not something that a student will overcome as they grow older. One father recounted the following story:

> Brian is a poster child, so to speak, for what you have found in your research. He is now 17 years old, has ADHD and has displayed the exact same inability to learn and retain classroom information that

[you] talk about in your studies. He feels stupid because he cannot read books and retain the information. He does okay on homework assignments but fails miserably on final exams. He has little if any ability to recall details on most subjects.

Persistent ADHD has an impact not only on their college grades, but their future employment prospects as well. Research has shown that adults with ADHD have a harder time in the workplace, shorter terms of employment, and commit more antisocial behavior, including theft and disorderly conduct (Alloway et al., 2013). Their poor working memory persists as well, which may explain the negative outcomes in adults with ADHD. Unable to control errant thoughts or impulsive behaviors using their working memory, they give in to them – committing inappropriate behaviors – and can't focus on their job tasks.

HOW: Strategies to support working memory

Two types of strategies are discussed here: **general working memory strategies** that can be applied to students with general learning needs and **specific working memory strategies** for students with ADHD. While the general strategies below are tailored for those with behavioral problems, you can modify them as appropriate for other students in your classroom.

General strategies

Shorten instructions to reduce the working memory load. In Chapter 1 we learned the average working memory capacity for each age group. Keep this in mind when working with a student with ADHD. Start with the average limit for a particular age group, then give the student with ADHD one or two items less than that to reduce the working memory load for them:

- For students younger than 8 years old, give them 1 to 2 steps
- For students between the ages of 8 and 10 years, give them 2 to 3 steps
- For students between the ages of 11 and 13 years, give them 3 to 4 steps

Shorten study periods or activities to reduce the working memory load. When activities are broken up with a break in the middle, it makes it easier for the ADHD student to stay on track. Timed bursts of effort, such as 5–10 minutes, are better than a prolonged length of time. If the class is spending 20 minutes reading, the student with ADHD should spend 8 minutes reading, then take a 3-minute break and come back to complete the reading.

Psychologists describe the way in which we remember things as being like a 'U' shape – we remember things at the beginning of a list because we have had an opportunity to repeat it over and over. We also remember things at the end of the list because we just heard them. But information in the middle of the list (the dip in the 'U') often gets forgotten. While most of us find it hard to keep track of what was said in the middle of the list, the student with ADHD finds it especially difficult. They lose information because they can't simultaneously maintain their attention on a task and use their working memory to process the information the teacher is giving them.

Repeat information intermittently to boost working memory. When we rehearse information, we are more likely to remember it. However, the way in which we rehearse the information is important. It is much more effective to rehearse information *intermittently*, rather than at a set time each week. If a student is revising for an exam, one way to reinforce the information is to test them periodically.

Pop quizzes are a great way to test them. Studies have found that even if feedback is not provided, the student is more likely to remember the information than if they just revised the text on their own. The act of thinking about the material encourages a deeper processing and engagement with lessons.

Specific strategies

Use a visual timer. Students with ADHD have a hard time keeping track of time or managing their own schedule, so provide something bold that they can see.

Reward frequently and intermittently. If you are using a token system to reward students with ADHD, offer rewards frequently and intermittently. These students have difficulty with *delayed gratification* – they would rather receive a small incentive now than a bigger one later.

Encode the environment. Teach students to use environmental cues to support working memory. First, ask them to think of where they were when they learnt the information they are trying to remember. What chair were they sitting on? Were they wearing their favorite shirt? What song were they listening to? What time of day was it? Cues in the physical environment can trigger their working memory and prevent them from abandoning classroom activities when they become too difficult.

Jump for working memory! Research has confirmed that when students are more physically involved with learning, the easier it is to recall that information. Make it easier for students with ADHD to recall information by having them perform a physical activity while learning. For example, if the class is learning about how the Egyptians built the pyramids, have them make pulling motions to remember how the heavy stones were pulled up an incline, and pushing motions to remember how they were pushed into place.

Because many things do not have an explicit action associated with them – like sentence diagramming – a student's actions do not always need to match what they are learning. For a less explicitly 'active' lesson, they may want to jump up at the first part of the lesson, then fold their arms, and then cross their legs. The important thing is that you help them connect the action with the information. Then, when they need to recall the information, you can ask them to perform the action in order to trigger their memory.

Science Flash: Rewiring the brain?

Neurofeedback, also known as biofeedback, is a method of providing real-time information on how the brain functions using EEG. The goal is to encourage students with ADHD to increase their production of beta waves (more beta waves result in attentive behavior) and to suppress the production of theta waves (linked to daydreaming). Usually, when a student with ADHD is given an attention task they increase their theta waves instead of beta waves. Neurofeedback is a technique to train them to increase beta waves and inhibit their brain's production of theta waves. By giving them immediate feedback on their brainwave patterns, they learn to make this adjustment. As a result, they show an improvement in cognitive skills and attention.

Neurofeedback has been used successfully in those with epilepsy; however, there are problems with the results relating to individuals with ADHD. Although there are published studies reporting positive effects of neurofeedback on individuals with ADHD, these have been considered as unreliable because of small sample size, lack of control groups, and experimenters who are not 'blind' to participant treatment status. Another criticism is that many of the individuals included in these studies may not even have had a diagnosis of ADHD. Furthermore, only 50% of patients seem to benefit and, unfortunately, the child has to undergo a substantial number of trials before this is evident. Finally, we don't know if there are any harmful effects of manipulating brainwave patterns in children. While neurofeedback offers an alternative to medication for children with ADHD, more research is necessary to validate the effectiveness of this treatment.

Case Study: Stephen – combined ADHD profile

Stephen's behaviors in relation to *DSM-5*:

- Often does not seem to listen when spoken to directly
- Is often forgetful in daily activities
- Often runs about or climbs in situations where it is not appropriate
- Often blurts out an answer before a question has been completed
- Often interrupts or intrudes on others (e.g., butts into conversations or games)

Stephen, 10 years old, was consistently struggling with his schoolwork. In class, he often drifted off into deep thought, or I would catch him sneaking cars from the toy bin in the room. He used these toys to keep himself occupied during lessons, rolling the cars around on his lap, or on top of his desk. When I called on him to answer a question, he usually responded before I finished asking the question. When class assignments were given, he forgot what he was supposed to do. When I restated the directions, he didn't pay attention.

Another problem was his social relationships. When it was time for recess, he pushed his way to the front of the line, angering his fellow classmates. On the playground, he climbed trees and ran around continuously, ignoring the teachers who told him to stop. If he did stop, he imposed himself into the other students' activities, often interrupting games of hide and seek by running around and finding everyone before the designated 'finder' had a chance. This behavior often caused arguments between Stephen and his peers, and prevented him from forming friendships with his classmates.

Strategies

- Minimize distractions so working memory is not overwhelmed

I moved Stephen to the front of the class where there were fewer distractions for him. I also maintained eye contact whenever I gave him instructions. This meant that Stephen's working memory did not have to work overtime to inhibit his impulsive behavior.

- Shorten instructions to reduce the working memory load

Stephen also had a problem listening in class, so I began asking him shorter questions and verbally rewarded him if he did not interrupt. If he did interrupt or got the wrong answer, I simply restated the question until he was able to answer it correctly.

- Break down information to reduce working memory processing

I also gave him simple questions, like 'There are 3 apples in a basket and you ate 2 of them, how many do you have left?' I then walked him through the steps of the question so he could understand the process. This turned out to be beneficial for the entire class as the detailed explanations also helped the other students retain the information.

- Repeat information to boost working memory

I also encouraged Stephen to repeat the question back to me, to ensure that he was paying attention, as well as to allow him to verbalize and understand the information.

- Shorten study periods to reduce the working memory load

To make it easier for Stephen to stay on track, I allowed him to take frequent breaks during his class activities. I asked him to stand and stretch to release some energy. This allowed him to get out his 'wiggles' and focus on his classwork after his break.

- Reward intermittently

For recess, I also incorporated shortened activities. Stephen had to choose a short play activity with other students and stick with it. If he stayed with that group, I allowed the entire class extra playtime on an intermittent basis. If he left his group, he had to stand next to me until the end of recess.

Over time, he was able to control his impulses and made friends with classmates that he played with every day. With patience and consistent reinforcement, Stephen was able to drastically improve over the school year, becoming calmer and performing better on assessments.

Case Study: Susan – hyperactive behaviors

Susan's behaviors in relation to *DSM-5*:

- Often fidgets with or taps hands or feet, or squirms in seat
- Often leaves seat in situations when remaining seated is expected
- Often talks excessively

(Continued)

(Continued)

- Often has trouble waiting her turn
- Often unable to play or take part in leisure activities quietly
- Is often 'on the go', acting as if 'driven by a motor'

Susan, 14 years old, had been having a number of behavioral problems at school, often ending up in time-out or in the principal's office. When Susan first came to my class I was surprised she was not more popular. She had traits similar to other social students – she was extroverted in her conversation, often talking excitedly and loudly. The reading class that she was in required her to be able to read independently for periods as long as 30 minutes. During these 30-minute reading sessions, each student was allowed to pick a spot in the room to read, on beanbags, chairs, or the carpet, and stay there in silence for the duration of the exercise. Susan had trouble choosing a spot in the room and sticking to it. For instance, she would start in her seat, and move on to a beanbag, then end up on the carpet. Even when she settled on a spot for more than 10 minutes, her knee was always bouncing and she moved around constantly in her seat, as if she were uncomfortable. This pattern disturbed the students around her.

For the class reading exercise, each student was assigned a portion of the text to read. Susan often started reading during someone else's turn or she lost track of her place in the book. When it was time to listen to an audio book, she talked constantly to the students around her. As a result, she was removed from the classroom until the book finished. However, this meant that she was unfamiliar with the story and could not work on the book report based on the audio.

She also took multiple bathroom breaks during the 50-minute reading class and I often found her sitting outside of the classroom instead of going to the washroom. As a result of her behavioral issues, her grades were low, particularly in reading.

Strategies

- Shorten activities to reduce the working memory load

I began by shortening the number of pages Susan had to read. I rewarded her on a chart each time she finished her assigned reading.

- Minimize distractions so working memory is not overwhelmed

I also limited the number of options of places to sit during reading time. For instance, I only allowed her to move three times in the first few weeks, then two times, then once, and eventually she was not allowed to move at all. This strategy eventually made her feel more at ease staying in one spot during the quiet reading time.

• Reward frequently

I also offered Susan extra credit for reading more than I requested during quiet reading time. Since her grades were so poor, this was good motivation for her to sit down and read.

• Shorten activities to reduce the working memory load

During book listening time, I stopped the story every 10 minutes and discussed what was just presented, making sure to ask questions and engage Susan directly. This helped her stay on task instead of talking to other students.

• Use visual representation to support working memory

During class reading times, I wrote down who was responsible for reading different parts of the book on the board. This allowed Susan to keep up with the class. When it was Susan's turn to read, she was able to start without prompting.

• Keep track of her place in complex activities

I also taught Susan how to keep track of her place in the book by using an unsharpened pencil to follow each sentence as it was being read aloud by another student. This meant that her working memory was free to focus on understanding the text rather than trying to find her place in the story.

• Minimize distractions so working memory is not overwhelmed

In order to keep her inside the classroom rather than sitting outside, I limited her bathroom breaks to only one per class. I also used the buddy system to hold her accountable for going to the washroom and coming straight back to the classroom. Over a period of a few months, Susan was able to follow along in the book, read independently at reading times, and perform well on reading-based assignments.

Case Study: David – inattention behaviors

David's behaviors in relation to *DSM-5*:

- Often fails to give close attention to details or makes careless mistakes in schoolwork, at work, or with other activities
- Often has trouble holding attention on tasks or play activities
- Often does not follow through on instructions, and fails to finish schoolwork, chores, or duties in the workplace (e.g., loses focus, side-tracked)
- Often avoids, dislikes, or is reluctant to do tasks that require mental effort over a long period of time (such as schoolwork or homework)
- Is often easily distracted
- Is often forgetful in daily activities

At 11 years old, most boys can focus their attention long enough to be successful in a classroom setting. However, David is not a typical 11-year-old boy. His grades in all his classes, outside of physical education, were extremely poor. He had a problem following directions and finishing his work. Every morning, before we started learning new material, we reviewed the previous day's work. Students then took out their notebooks to write an essay on the work that we had done. David could not seem to remember to get his notebook before he sat down at his desk. He used to forget his notebook at home, but I asked the students to leave their notebooks in their cubbies. David still forgot to bring it to his desk and the class had to wait for him before they began the writing activity.

Often, David did not even complete his work, and argued with me instead. An instance of this was when I gave the class a math assignment relating to the class lesson. When I was teaching the lesson, I noticed him fiddling with his pencil, sliding it across his desk, and looking away from me. When he had to complete the worksheet reviewing the lesson, he had no idea what to do as he had not been paying attention.

Instead of working, he often doodled on his worksheet. Sometimes the students had multiple worksheets to complete and I instructed them to finish one before moving on to the next. David would complete a single problem on each worksheet, and then it would be full of doodles.

He also did not follow instructions. For instance, when he had a math worksheet, I instructed him to show each step of the problem in order to make sure he was following the correct steps. David would get the correct answer 50% of the time, but did not show his work so I could correct his errors.

Strategies

- Use visual representation to support working memory

During my lesson, I started using presentations with pictures, and sometimes videos, on the whiteboard to engage David's attention.

- Minimize distractions so working memory is not overwhelmed

I also removed all pictures and signs from the front of the classroom so the only form of stimulation at the front was the information I was presenting. David responded well to this and seemed more attentive.

- Keep track of his place in complex activities

To combat his pencil play, I passed out note-taking papers with fill-in-the-blanks to accompany my lesson. An example of this was a presentation slide that said, 'A point is a single, exact location in space', and a worksheet that said, 'A point is _____'. This active engagement helped David keep track of the lesson, as well as better absorb the information.

- Break down explanations to reduce working memory processing

During the math exercises, I sat next to David and broke down the problem into smaller steps. For instance, when we were reviewing the length of the hypotenuse of a right-angled triangle, I drew the triangle on his paper so he could visualize the problem: 'Side A = 5, side B = 10. What is side C?' We worked through this problem step by step so that he could solve it correctly.

- Shorten activities to reduce the working memory load

I only gave David one worksheet at a time. Once he completed a worksheet, I gave him the next one. If he did not finish all the worksheets, he had to do them as homework and he lost points for that lesson. Over the next few weeks, he was able to focus on his work and accomplish it during class time without losing any points.

Summary

1. **Core deficit**: Students with ADHD have difficulties inhibiting behavior, which may manifest itself as trouble in controlling actions and emotions at school.

(Continued)

(Continued)

2. **Working memory profile**: These students have impairments in both verbal and visual–spatial working memory, but *visual–spatial working memory* is most affected.
3. **Strategies**: Support these students by giving shorter instructions and activities; and reduce working memory processing in classroom activities.

Note

1. One concern about the use of teacher checklists is the degree to which such evaluations are susceptible to a negative halo effect, where some behaviors have a greater impact upon teacher evaluations than others. For example, disruptive behaviors such as defiance towards a teacher are more likely to result in the child being rated as both hyperactive and inattentive, despite there being an absence of attention problems on their part. However, numerous studies (including, for example, Alloway, Elliott, and Holmes, 2010), have demonstrated that there is a high correspondence between teacher ratings and standardized cognitive tests, with teachers demonstrating high levels of classification accuracy of attention problems.

References and further reading

Alloway, T.P. (2011) A comparison of WM profiles in children with ADHD and DCD. *Child Neuropsychology*, 21: 1–12.

Alloway, T.P. and Cockcroft, K. (2012) Working memory in ADHD: a comparison of British and South African children. *Journal of Attention Disorders*. DOI: 10.1177/108705471141739.

Alloway, T.P. and Elsworth, M. (2012) An investigation of cognitive skills and behavior in high-ability students. *Learning and Individual Differences*, 22: 891–5.

Alloway, T.P. and Stein, A. (2014) Investigating the link between cognitive skills and learning in non-comorbid samples of ADHD and SLI. *International Journal of Educational Research*, 64: 26–31.

Alloway, T.P., Gathercole, S.E, Kirkwood, H.J., and Elliott, J.E. (2009a) The cognitive and behavioral characteristics of children with low working memory. *Child Development*, 80: 606–21.

Alloway, T.P., Gathercole, S., Holmes, J., Place, M., and Elliott, J. (2009b) The diagnostic utility of behavioral checklists in identifying children with ADHD and children with working memory deficits. *Child Psychiatry & Human Development*, 40: 353–66.

Alloway, T.P., Rajendran, G., and Archibald, L.M. (2009) Working memory profiles of children with developmental disorders. *Journal of Learning Difficulties*, 42: 372–82.

Alloway, T.P., Elliott, J., and Holmes, J. (2010) The prevalence of ADHD-like symptoms in a community sample. *Journal of Attention Disorders*, 14: 52–6.

Alloway, T.P., Elliott, J., and Place, M. (2010) Investigating the relationship between attention and working memory in clinical and community samples. *Child Neuropsychology*, 16: 242–54.

Alloway, T.P., Gathercole, S.E., and Elliott, J. (2010) Examining the link between working memory behavior and academic attainment in children with ADHD. *Developmental Medicine & Child Neurology*, 52: 632–6.

Alloway, T.P., Lawrence, A., and Rodgers, S. (2013) Antisocial behavior: exploring behavioral, cognitive and environmental influences on expulsion. *Applied Cognitive Psychology*, 27: 520–6.

Alloway, T.P., Elsworth, M., Miley, N., and Sekinger, S. (2014). Computer use and behavior problems in twice-exceptional students. *Gifted Education International.*

Barkley, R. (2006) *Attention-Deficit Hyperactivity Disorder: A Handbook for Diagnosis and Treatment*, 3rd edition. New York: Guilford Press.

Barkley, R., Murphy, K., and Kwasnik, D. (1996) Psychological adjustment and adaptive impairments in young adults with ADHD. *Journal of Attention Disorders,* 1: 41–54.

CDC (Centers for Disease Control and Prevention) (2013) Attention-deficit hyperactivity disorder: data and statistics. www.cdc.gov/ncbddd/adhd/data.html (retrieved February 2014).

Gathercole, S.E, Alloway, T.P., Kirkwood, H.J., and Elliott, J.E. (2008) Attentional and executive function behaviors in children with poor working memory. *Learning and Individual Differences*, 18: 214–23.

Holmes, J., Gathercole, S., Place, M., Alloway, T.P., and Elliott, J. (2010) An assessment of the diagnostic utility of EF assessments in the identification of ADHD in children. *Child & Adolescent Mental Health*, 15: 37–43.

Reiss, M.J. (1993) Organizing and running a residential fieldtrip. *School Science Review*, 74: 132–5.

CHAPTER 7

AUTISTIC SPECTRUM DISORDER (ASD)

This chapter looks at:

- WHAT is autism?
- WHERE are the affected brain regions?
- WHY is working memory linked to autistic spectrum disorder (ASD)?
- HOW can working memory be supported in students with ASD?

'But the dinosaurs died a long time ago.' It was the third time in under a minute that Mark, 12 years old, had made that observation. The class were discussing what a boy who travels through time to explore the Cretaceous period might see, but Mark was unable to imagine that a human could ever see a live dinosaur. When Mr Kim, the science teacher, challenged students with new information, or approached familiar information in a creative manner, Mark often disagreed and became frustrated. His class-mates struggled with his behavior, particularly when undertaking group projects, like the time they had to recreate the solar system. When every-one was ready to move on to drawing Mars after drawing the Earth, Mark was complaining that the drawing of the continent of South America was too small on the picture of the Earth.

Socially, too, Mark had a hard time shifting between the nuances of the playground and the classroom, sometimes raising his hand to get a friend's attention on the swing, and becoming upset when they didn't acknowledge him, or shouting in the classroom when he had a point to make, as if he were outside. Mark's struggle to use flexible thinking to appropriately adapt to the context was also evident in his grades. While he excelled at math, with its absolute and unchanging rules (like 36 squared always equals 1269), he had a much harder time with literature, which required him to deal with abstract and hard-to-pin-down texts.

WHAT it is

Autism is characterized by a difficulty to recognize and respond appropriately to social and emotional cues, which causes problems with social interactions. Autism is a spectrum disorder, which means that some of these students will grow up into adults who are able to function normally in daily life and are indistinguishable from their peers, while others need continued support even for simple daily activities, such as going out shopping or to work.

Try It: Theory of mind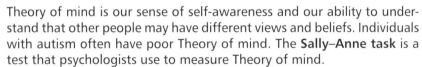

Theory of mind is our sense of self-awareness and our ability to understand that other people may have different views and beliefs. Individuals with autism often have poor Theory of mind. The **Sally–Anne task** is a test that psychologists use to measure Theory of mind.

You can try this on a young child. Take two dolls and call them 'Sally' and 'Anne'. Show the child that Sally puts a marble in a basket in the room and then leaves. Tell the child that Anne decides to play a trick on Sally so she moves the marble from the basket into a box. Now ask the child where they think Sally will look for the marble when she comes back into the room.

Their response reveals whether or not they are aware of other people's perspectives. If the child realizes that Sally will look for the marble in the basket and not the box, then they are able to adopt Sally's perspective.

(Continued)

(Continued)

Their response will depend on their age. Most typically developing children under 4 years will say that Sally will look in the box. By 5 years of age, most will be able adopt Sally's perspective and pass this task. However, the majority of individuals with autism will fail this task even in their teenage years (Happe, 1995).

In addition to the social difficulties that accompany autism, their cognitive skills are greatly impaired. Sometimes the simplest activities in the classroom can prove challenging for them. However, students with autism can demonstrate remarkable abilities in some tasks while struggling in others. Other children, like Mark, have an average intelligence and so are expected to achieve average academic outcomes. However, because of their autism, they struggle to do so. Students with autism are identified on a spectrum from high functioning to low functioning. IQ plays an important role in determining where an individual falls in this spectrum. High-functioning students have a higher IQ score (IQ scores greater than 70), while low-functioning students have such a low IQ score (IQ scores lower than 70) that it is at the same level as an individual with a severe intellectual disability. However, IQ does not tell the whole story. This chapter looks at the missing piece in the puzzle – working memory – to explain the discrepancy between IQ and grades.

Communication difficulties are most evident in the classroom. In a small percentage of cases, individuals with low-functioning ASD can be classified as nonverbal and may not use language to express their needs. This type of student usually acts out in frustration. For example, they may throw their books and pencils on the floor because they find it hard to communicate that they don't like group work. Other characteristics include echolalia, where the student will reproduce phrases that they have heard in an unrelated context to express their emotions or respond to a question in class. Alice, who works with the National Autistic Society (in the UK), described how one boy used *Thomas the Tank Engine* to communicate that he felt angry that day: 'Thomas was having a bad day. Henry was on his tracks.' Students may also repeat phrases from their home life to contribute to the classroom. For example, they may describe a scene from their favorite cartoon during science class. Although the information may not be relevant, they are trying to find the right words to be part of the activity.

Their understanding of language can also be very literal, a feature that even high-functioning ASD individuals can display. A comment like

'Don't run in the hallway' can bring the student with ASD to a complete halt, instead of slowing them down to walk. Individuals with ASD have been described as lacking social instinct. They need clear rules in order to function and often show inflexibility in understanding when you can bend these rules. For example, the concept of personal space can change with the context, so they don't understand that it is okay to stand close to someone on a crowded bus, but not when the bus is empty. Alice, at the National Autistic Society, compares their social impairment to a car that encounters a fallen tree in its path. The typical child is like a 4×4 truck that can drive around the tree to carry on to its destination. The child with ASD is like a small car that is stuck at that tree because they can't go around it. They have to wait for someone to come to remove the tree from their path before they can continue. School is full of trees in the road – social encounters that require an implicit and creative response to complex situations. The student with ASD is often not equipped with the social skills to drive around them.

DSM and diagnosis

Deficits of ASD include:

- Social–emotional reciprocity (example: unable to initiate conversation or share interests)
- Deficits in nonverbal communicative behaviors used for social interaction (lack of eye contact, abnormalities in body)
- Deficits in developing, maintaining, and understanding relationships

These children also show restricted or repetitive patterns of behavior, interests, or activities (example: lining up toys or flipping objects, inflexible adherence to routines, adverse response to specific sounds or textures). Asperger's syndrome is now combined with the diagnosis of ASD in *DSM-5*.

A diagnosis of autistic spectrum disorder (ASD) can reliably be made as early as 2 or 3 years of age by various health professionals. A pediatrician will conduct a semi-structured interview, as well as a diagnostic interview, with the parents. They can also make sure that developmental milestones such as motor skills, hand–eye coordination, pretend play, and related social skills are met. A speech therapist can also detect whether the child's language skills are lagging behind their peers.

(Continued)

(Continued)

A commonly used tool is the Autism Diagnostic Observation Schedule (ADOS), which assesses skills in communication, social interaction, and play. A diagnosis of ASD is usually made over a number of sessions so that the clinician has an opportunity to observe the child in a variety of situations. Medical and family history may be requested to complement the cognitive, behavioral, and language assessments.

WHERE it is: Working memory and the autistic brain

The brain of a child with autism develops differently from children without it. Recent research has found that the prefrontal cortex (PFC), the home of working memory, is one of the brain regions most affected by autism. Initial results show that the PFC of a child with autism has a much greater volume of neurons, up to 67% more. One possible explanation for this excess growth is that the genes controlling neuron development are overactive, resulting in the greater brain volume. Exactly how this is related to autistic behavior is unclear at the moment, but the link between an abnormal PFC and autism suggests that there may be a working memory connection to the behavior (Courchesne and Pierce, 2005).

Children with autism also display less activation in the PFC when they are asked to remember and process information. This pattern seems to be evident regardless of the nature of the task. In one experiment they were asked to process letters, in another experiment, shapes, and in another, faces. In all instances, the result was the same: there was less activation in the PFC for children with autism than in those without it. The study with faces also found that children with autism tend to analyse facial features like objects, rather than in light of social relationships, which may be related to their trouble interpreting social nuances (Koshino et al., 2005, 2008).

Furthermore, when a child with ASD is presented with two tasks and has to focus on one while ignoring the other distracting task, their brain activity reveals that they do not actually shift their attention to the more important information (Luna et al., 2002). They have a difficult time determining what information is important. In the classroom, some students with ASD might appear to struggle with certain memory-heavy activities. However, this may be connected to their difficulty in knowing what they should focus on, rather than a working memory deficit *per se.*

WHY working memory is linked to autism

The working memory profile of the student with ASD depends on whether they are low or high functioning. In some cases, high-functioning students can have an above average verbal working memory, while low-functioning students perform at the same level as a student with a specific language impairment. In general, low-functioning ASD students also have a poorer working memory than their typically developing peers do.

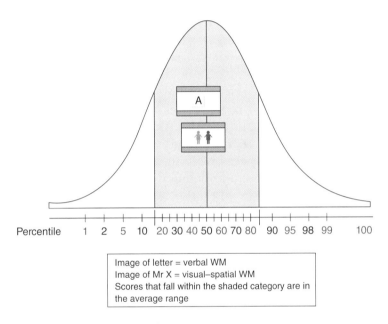

Figure 7.1 Working memory profile in ASD

However, even high-functioning ASD students can display verbal working memory problems. Research has shown that the type of material they have to remember provides us with a clue to their working memory profile (Alloway et al., 2009). They struggle in particular with abstract information like nonsense words or new vocabulary. Why? One explanation is that when they are presented with abstract ideas that they have to both process and remember, they spend too long trying to comprehend the material and so forget what they need to do. For example, during a verbal working memory test (Listening Recall test in the Try It box in Chapter 1), Daniel, a 14-year-old with ASD, was presented with the sentence *Dogs can play the guitar*. Daniel spent a long time thinking about the sentence before finally answering 'True', because 'you can train a dog'. As a result of the lengthy time spent deliberating on the answer, he forgot the final word in the list of sentences (Alloway et al., 2009).

The strategies they use to remember information can also overburden them. Studies confirm that when remembering information, high-functioning ASD individuals do not use their long-term memory, visual strategies, or even contextual clues. Instead, they rehearse things over and over again. While this can be useful in remembering short sequences of information, it is ultimately a time-consuming and inefficient strategy to simply keep repeating things. These students are aware of their own memory problems. Alistair, a high-functioning 13-year-old, commented that he had 'number overload' when he failed a test that required him to repeat numbers in backwards order.

Now, let's look at their visual–spatial working memory profile. The majority of individuals with ASD do not have deficits in this area. Take the Dot Matrix test from the AWMA as an example. In this task, students are shown a matrix with dots that appear in random locations and they have to recall their location in a backwards sequence. Personal research as well as other studies confirm that students with ASD do as well as their peers without autism. In the classroom this means they should be able to remember information that is presented visually. The problem arises when they have to shift between looking at the teacher talking and the information written on the blackboard, and as a result, they can find it hard to remember the lesson even if it is presented visually.

Working memory and savants

What does working memory look like in savants? Some autistic savants can display amazing abilities well beyond their age, yet struggle in simple, everyday tasks. One teacher recalled a 12-year-old boy who loved going to the principal's office to work on math and science exams for 17-year-olds, but could not dress himself. These abilities far exceed expectations based on their IQ, and in some cases, their giftedness exceeds the level reached by experts in the same field. Their special abilities are generally found in the domains of music, memorization of lists, three-dimensional drawing, reading (hyperlexia), and calendar and mental calculation (see Science Flash).

Does their working memory reflect their extraordinary skills? It depends on the working memory task. If the working memory task uses material that is related to their area of expertise, then savants outperform individuals with ASD without special abilities. For example, a savant calculator has a much higher score than ASD non-experts in number-based working memory tasks. However, the savants will perform similarly as ASD non-experts in a working memory task that uses shapes.

Autistic savants have built up a huge knowledge base that can be used to increase working memory performance in the area of their expertise. In some cases, their expertise and training in one area can also enhance their scores in another area. For example, calendar calculators and savant calculators can achieve phenomenal scores in memory tests using nonsense words. They are able to apply their training in remembering one type of abstract material (dates and numbers) to related things.

Science Flash: The *Rain Man* effect

An autistic savant is someone who is autistic with a special skill, usually related to memory. For example, they might be able to draw an accurate replication of a scene or location after looking at it for just a few minutes. Another example is an amazing ability to perform complicated math problems in their head or tell you what day it was on 25 February, 1869 (calendar calculating). A child who has savant abilities would draw three-dimensional pictures while their friends were scribbling. They might be able to put together a jigsaw puzzle that adults struggle doing, without even looking at the picture. Their exceptional memory helps them recognize patterns in things that would take the average adult ages to figure out.

In an odd twist of nature, autistic savants have such specialized skills because part of their brain is damaged: the left hemisphere that deals with language and processing information. This damage leads to learning disabilities and difficulty coping in everyday situations. To deal with this damage, the right side of their brain is unlocked, resulting in a 'spotlight' on one of the five senses. If there is a spotlight on hearing, for example, then the autistic savant has amazing musical skills.

Is there a *Rain Main* hiding in us all? Scientists have used special technology to temporarily immobilize the same part of the brain in healthy adults. The volunteers showed incredible skills similar to autistic savants, such as naming the day when given a date in history and drawing abilities.

HOW: Strategies to support working memory

Two types of strategies are discussed here: **general working memory strategies** that can be applied to students with general learning needs, and **specific working memory strategies** for students with ASD. While the general strategies below are tailored for those with ASD, you can modify them as appropriate for other students in your classroom.

General strategies

Break down information to reduce working memory processing. Students with ASD find multi-tasking (like listening to a lesson while taking notes) difficult because they expend so much effort in shifting their attention from one task to another that it overloads their working memory. Consequently, they fail to complete both activities correctly. Avoid this by giving them one activity at a time: listen to the lecture, and then write notes based on what they learned.

Reduce working memory processing in activities. The type of lesson can make a difference in how students with ASD process and remember information. They find it difficult to complete assignments with abstract concepts or topics that don't have a clear right or wrong answer and where they have to express their views. One parent described his son, Brodie, a 10-year-old with ASD: 'He needs to understand why "A" leads to "B" before he will accept it. This has left him little capacity for the more mundane, functional literacy elements.'

Where possible, provide as much structure or rule-based learning for the student with ASD as you can. A science teacher described how Joseph hated it when she introduced a debate on ethical issues like 'What are the implications of cloning?' So she allowed him to opt out of such discussions and spend his time writing a short essay on the process of cloning instead. This provided him with a clear structure of what to do and still allowed him to learn about cloning.

Minimize distractions so working memory is not overwhelmed. Students with ASD can have an adverse response to certain physical stimuli and can be overwhelmed by different sensory inputs like light, noise, and heat. While this does not directly relate to working memory problems, these issues can be a trigger that overloads their senses, making it difficult for them to use their working memory to process new information. Thus, a few extra minutes spent each day doing a quick check on the classroom environment can make a big difference for the student with ASD. First, check the lighting – is it bright enough? Make sure that windows or areas that let in light do not have posters or charts covering them. If you have a student who is sensitive to light, consider moving them away from a window.

Noise is another issue for students with ASD. Check where they are seated – is it close to a window? Are they at the back of the class where it is too noisy? Malcolm, a teacher in the UK, found that when he gave his ASD student the option to use headphones during individual work, his behavior improved dramatically. He did not act out in frustration as much and could finish his work quickly.

Students with ASD can be easily distracted and they tend to fixate on the distraction, thus using their working memory space. Try to remove classroom distractions. Is the solar system mobile hanging too low and near their desk? Is the room cluttered? Can they find a tidy place to work on their own?

Specific strategies

Minimize physical overstimulation so working memory is not overwhelmed. Students with ASD may also experience discomfort in the classroom if they are hypersensitive to certain materials touching their skin. Allow them to take their shoes off in class or give them a cushion for their chair. These simple steps can create a more productive environment that will allow the student with ASD to use their working memory efficiently.

Set routines. Students with ASD are drawn to routine and structure. While we all have our idiosyncrasies around which way the toilet paper is placed or whether we pour our milk or coffee first, the student with ASD usually cannot function unless these structures are in place. They are easily upset if something in the classroom is out of its assigned location or placed haphazardly and their attention is shifted to this instead. When there is structure in place in the classroom, their working memory and attention can focus on the task at hand instead.

Connect new information with their interests. Capitalize on a student's interest or expertise, whether it is about dinosaurs or the solar system, and use it to promote learning. For example, if a student knows all about tractors, ask him whether the letters that he is struggling to learn look like parts of a tractor. Develop his ability to create such connections on his own. This process helps working memory shift new information to long-term knowledge more quickly. The student can then use their working memory to work with that knowledge, like write a word using the letters that they were previously struggling to learn.

Current Debate: Does technology challenge or cripple students with autism?

In the past few years there has been the introduction of new technology. Everything from computers to cell phones has evolved to become more accessible and more efficient. Their ease of use has allowed many therapists and behaviorists to implement technology in clinics and classrooms. The 'tablet' is the most commonly used device in the autistic community. It is small, capable of multiple useful functions, easy to

(Continued)

(Continued)

transport, and is not complicated for a child to learn to use. Since the recent spike in popularity, a lot of parents and clinicians have become concerned about the costs and benefits for an autistic child who's using it. Below is a quick breakdown of both sides of the argument.

The Benefits: Most tablets offer applications (commonly referred to as 'apps') that support verbal, visual, and tactile capabilities in young children. Some of these apps help children learn to read and write, while others encourage imaginative play. Parents whose children use these devices rave about their children making great strides in these areas.

The Costs: The first cost is the large price tag. These devices can cost up to and over US$800. Aside from the high cost, it is also a useless tool if the child is not under proper supervision. There is the risk too of overstimulation. The tablet can take over normal social interaction and hurt children with an already delayed social ability. The tablet can become an obsession for some children, and they can grow entirely dependent on the device.

Do the costs outweigh the benefits? This differs for each child, as each child has his or her own needs. If a child is a visual learner, then a tablet device is a great option to be used in concordance with other activities. If a child has fine motor difficulties, or self-harming behavior, it may not be best to give them a device that they will not be able to use, or may break. It is also important to remember that no device should be implemented without proper supervision to prevent excessive use and dependence.

Case Study: Tommy – low-functioning ASD

Tommy's behaviors in relation to *DSM-5*:

- Deficits in social–emotional reciprocity
- Deficits in nonverbal communicative behaviors used for social interactions
- Hyper- or hypo-reactivity to sensory input or unusual interests in sensory aspects of the environment

Tommy, 15 years old, was a very low-functioning ASD student attending a school designed to support the needs of autistic children. His classroom consisted of five ASD students, a teacher, and a counselor. I worked with Tommy every morning for several hours. His verbal skills were poor and our conversations were typically one-sided. For example, when I asked him how his weekend was, he talked about his older siblings instead. Even when I tried to bring the conversation back to what he did over the weekend, he carried on talking about his family as if he didn't hear me.

He was often asked to complete complex work in a short period of time. For example, his morning consisted of copying multiple sentences in plain writing and in cursive. In one activity he had to write his address, '1324 Drury Lane, Argleton, Massachusetts', five times in his notebook. This activity proved to be too difficult for him and he often displayed a glazed look.

Tommy's good performance in the classroom was rewarded using animals on a Velcro board. However, Tommy was often distracted by the animals on his board and spent class time staring at them instead of completing his work.

Strategies

- Set routines

I made a daily schedule for Tommy that remained the same. This allowed him to have certain expectations of what he needed to accomplish each day. Each morning began with a conversation, followed by him learning his address by writing sentences; then he moved on to the rest of his learning activities.

- Break down information to reduce working memory processing

For his sentences, I began teaching him the number of his house, '1324'. Once he was able to correctly write down this number sequence and repeat it to me from memory, we moved on to the next part of the address, 'Drury Lane'. I repeated this method for the next two pieces of information: his city 'Argleton' and state 'Massachusetts'. Instead of writing down his address on the top of his paper for him to copy, I prompted him, saying, 'What is your house number?' By the end of the month, I could ask him his address without any prompts and he was able to recite it.

- Minimize distractions so working memory is not overwhelmed

I moved all of the pictures around Tommy's desk so he would not be distracted. During our morning conversation, I sat directly in front of him so that he could focus on what I was saying. I also directed the morning conversation to the animals on the Velcro board, as he seemed very interested in them. He was able to carry on a conversation with me when we talked about the animals.

Case Study: Jeffry – low-functioning ASD

Jeffry's behaviors in relation to *DSM-5*:

- Deficits in social–emotional reciprocity
- Deficits in nonverbal communicative behaviors used for social interaction
- Deficits in developing, maintaining, and understanding relationships
- Stereotyped or repetitive motor movements or speech
- Highly restricted, fixated interests that are abnormal in intensity or focus

Jeffry, 12 years old, was on the autistic spectrum. Jeffry's most notable issue was with communication – he was completely nonverbal. When I talked directly to him he would not say a word, much less acknowledge what I said. Instead, he stared off into space and giggled. During a field trip, I noticed him covering his pants with both hands. I ran over and asked him whether he needed to use the bathroom. With a desperate look, he nodded his head and we made a mad dash to the bathroom.

When Jeffry became excited over something, he flailed his hands and arms. During a class visit to a museum, he ran around flailing, never staying at an exhibit for longer than a few seconds. He was more interested in the light switches at the museum than the exhibits themselves.

During playtime at school, Jeffry was given an iPad. While his peers were building toys together and talking, he played a building game on his iPad, completely absorbed in it. He did not have any friends in his class, as he was unwilling to communicate with them.

Strategies

- Break down explanations to reduce working memory processing

I worked to build Jeffry's communication skills by breaking down what he needed to do. I started by asking Jeffry simple questions, like 'Do you want to go to the washroom?' When he nodded, I let him know that he had to respond with a 'Yes'. After a few tries, he was able to say 'Yes', and after a few weeks he was able to ask 'Can I use the washroom, please?'

- Minimize physical overstimulation

Jeffry's flailing behavior occurred whenever he became overly excited. When this happened, I would ask him to have a quiet moment to collect his thoughts. I also encouraged him to hold his hands behind his back whenever he wanted to flail his arms. This helped him control his over-excitability and over time his flails were much shorter and less frequent.

- Minimize distractions so working memory is not overwhelmed

When I asked Jeffry why he was giggling randomly, his reasons varied from 'I don't know' to 'That poster is funny' (referring to one on the wall next to him). When I removed the distracting material from his immediate area, he seemed able to focus better, though he still required prompting in learning.

Over time he made friendships, was able verbalize thoughts, and control flailing impulses.

Case Study: Sarah – high-functioning ASD

Sarah's behaviors in relation to *DSM-5*:

- Stereotyped or repetitive motor movements or speech
- Highly restricted, fixated interests that are abnormal in intensity or focus

Sarah, 18 years old, was a high-functioning girl with ASD. Unlike most of the students in her class, she was able to work independently. I first noticed her abilities when I was working with her on a spelling assignment. She was memorizing a list of spelling words and began to list all the trains driving through her town. Her obsession with trains often distracted her from completing her class assignments. She could list off all of the train companies, names of the shipment organizations, and even tell me what routes a specific train took on any given day and time.

Another impressive sign of her memory was her ability to list off any *Star Trek* episode and the date it was released. Unfortunately her phenomenal ability to remember these things was not applicable to what she was learning in the classroom. Her narrow focus of interest crippled her in other topics in and out of the classroom. Although she was verbally proficient, most of our conversations were about whatever she was thinking of at the time, and she could not maintain a normal conversation if it didn't involve discussion about trains or *Star Trek*. For example, when I started talking to her about her dog, she told me about the new *Star Trek* movie instead.

(Continued)

(Continued)

Although Sarah performed well on memory-based assignments, like spelling, her math skills were similar to her lower-functioning ASD class-mates. She could spell complex and multisyllabic words, but couldn't do complex addition like '23 + 47' without prompting.

Despite her superior memory abilities she was often distracted during spelling tests and her performance suffered as a result. I would see her staring at her desk during the test, with her pencil sitting there, repeatedly making nonsense noises. This surprised me because she was really good at spelling. When I asked her about it, she said she didn't know how to start writing without any prompts.

Strategies

- Connect new information with their interests

I started connecting new information with topics that interested Sarah. For instance, on a math assignment where the question was 'What is 23 + 47?', I asked, 'If a train has 23 cargo containers and CSX (a train company) added 47 more, how many cargo containers does the train have now?' The train aspect of the story interested her, and made it easier for her to maintain focus on the question. I also encouraged her to form her own connections when she solved word problems.

- Break down information to reduce working memory processing

When Sarah struggled, I broke the problem (23 + 47) into smaller units, like 'What is 23 + 7?', then 'What is 30 + 40?' Soon she was able to solve multi-digit math problems without my prompts.

- Minimize distractions so working memory is not overwhelmed

Sarah's interest in trains and *Star Trek* often distracted her from her work. I decided to use this as a positive reinforcement. Whenever she stayed on task for the duration of the activity, I let her talk about trains and *Star Trek* for 10 minutes as a reward for doing good work.

Over time, she was able to work independently on assignments and perform well on them. She was also able to have a normal conversation and focus on classwork, without making repetitive noises or getting distracted.

Summary

1. **Learning difficulty**: Students with ASD have a triad of impairments in communication, imagination, and social skills.
2. **Working memory profile**: High-functioning students with ASD have an average working memory profile. Low-functioning students with ASD have impairments in *verbal working memory* profile that impact their language and communication skills.
3. **Strategies**: Give students one task at a time and simplify activities; also minimize distractions and physical overstimulation so working memory can be directed on schoolwork instead of the classroom environment.

References and further reading

Alloway, T.P., Rajendran, G., and Archibald, L.M. (2009) Working memory profiles of children with developmental disorders. *Journal of Learning Difficulties*, 42: 372–82.

Baron-Cohen, S. (1993) *Autism and Asperger Syndrome: The Facts.* Oxford: Oxford University Press.

Courchesne, E. and Pierce, K. (2005) Brain overgrowth in autism during a critical time in development: implications for frontal pyramidal neuron and interneuron development and connectivity. *International Journal of Developmental Neuroscience*, 23: 153–70.

Happe, F. (1995) The role of age and verbal ability in the theory-of-mind task performance of subjects with autism. *Child Development*, 66: 843–55.

Koshino, H., Carpenter, P., Minshew, N., Cherkassky, V., Keller, T., and Just, M. (2005) Functional connectivity in an fMRI working memory task in high-functioning autism. *Neuroimage*, 24: 810–21.

Koshino, H., Kana, R., Keller, T., Cherkassky, V., Minshew, N., and Just, M. (2008) fMRI investigation of working memory for faces in autism: visual coding and underconnectivity with frontal areas. *Cerebral Cortex*, 18: 289–300.

Luna, B., Minshew, N.J., Garver, K.E., Lazar, N.A., Thulborn, K.R., Eddy, W.F., and Sweeney, J. (2002) Neocortical system abnormalities in autism: an fMRI study of spatial working memory. *Neurology*, 59: 834–40.

CHAPTER 8

ANXIETY DISORDERS

Evan Copello

This chapter looks at:

- WHAT is anxiety?
- WHERE are the affected brain regions?
- WHY is working memory linked to anxiety?
- HOW can working memory be supported in students with anxiety?

Every morning when 10-year-old Nicole gets dropped off at her elementary school, she gets out of her mother's car and heads straight to class. Nicole keeps a small notebook of her assignments for homework and upcoming tests. Most students rely on constant reminders, but she likes to be sure she remembers everything she needs to do. She finishes all of her homework on time, often even turning it in early.

During the week of a test Nicole becomes nervous and can be found studying after school at the library while her friends are in the playground waiting for their parents to pick them up. On test days Nicole is nervous and spends any class downtime studying for the test. She even studies while her teacher is lecturing in the classroom. Nicole's test grades are the highest in her class and she receives top marks on all of her homework and class assignments.

WHAT it is

Although some may look at Nicole and think she pushes herself too hard, Nicole has a healthy level of anxiety. Her anxiety helps her maintain a state of readiness, and her preparation results in her above-average grades. There is a continuum for anxiety levels: on one end there is healthy anxiety, like Nicole's, that helps the individual succeed in daily tasks; and on the other end is an unhealthy expression or anxiety disorders. The threshold for a student with normal stress and an anxiety disorder is determined in part by the effect it has on daily activities. Nicole has a high threshold for stress and her anxiety enhances her academic performance. However, this is not often the case for the student with an anxiety disorder. These students have greater difficulty focusing on tasks in class, as well as in daily life. Their anxiety can overwhelm them and they struggle with remembering multiple pieces of information at a time as a result.

Case Study: Mike

Mike, 14 years old, is in his first year in high school. He is not doing well in any of his classes. He is noticeably quiet in his classes, and spends the class time staring off into space. On test days he skips class and hides out in the bathroom until the class period has ended. Since he misses his tests, he is doing poorly in school, which makes him feel even more stressed.

In science class Mike had to present a poster on the atom. When it was his turn to speak, he noticed a group of students laughing at the back of the room. They were looking at a picture on one of their phones, but Mike thought they were laughing at him. So he ran out of the room in the middle of his presentation.

Mike is an example of someone who has performance anxiety – an unhealthy level of anxiety that negatively affects his performance in school. He is caught in a vicious cycle. He avoids taking tests and doing class projects so he has bad grades in his classes, which in turn makes him more stressed out and more likely to avoid future assessments. Unlike Nicole, Mike has a lower threshold for anxiety, which has a negative impact on his grades.

Worry is the underlying feature of anxiety disorders. Worry can be characterized by frequent unease and allowing one's mind to dwell on problems. Excessive worry can overtake a person's thought process, a phenomenon referred to as an 'attentional bias' – you focus on something due to reoccurring thoughts. The worry can be so invasive that it takes center stage in cognitive activities, replacing other more important information. Anxiety bombards working memory, making it difficult to process multiple pieces of information at the same time. For instance, a highly anxious student who is taught how to multiply fractions may not be able to solve a problem after the lesson because they spent the whole session worrying about the new, harder material. Throughout the lesson, their mind was overtaken by excessive worry and they were not able to focus on learning the information.

Try It: Worry

Start counting backwards by 3s from 100, like 100, 97, 94, 91, 88, ...
While you are doing this, perform the math problems below. Try solving them in your head, and if you cannot, then use a pencil and a piece of paper.

$$985 + 437 \qquad 461 - 378$$

While you were counting in 3s, you were using a large amount of your mental capacity. When you had to solve the problems provided, you had to put extra effort in the process, more than you would have if you just had to do the math problem without counting backwards. This activity illustrates how anxiety 'takes up' working memory and prevents an individual from solving an activity that otherwise may have been easy.

The task in the Try It box resembles the working memory load that a student with an anxiety disorder experiences on a daily basis. They are constantly distracted by invasive thoughts, such as 'Will my mom pick me up today?', 'If I take this test, I am going to fail, and if I fail, everyone is going to make fun of me.' Or 'This work is too hard and I'll never learn it.' These worrisome thoughts prevent the student from committing their full attention to the lesson.

DSM and diagnosis

How can we determine if a student like Mike is struggling from an anxiety disorder, and how can we differentiate Mike's level of anxiety from Nicole's? In order to be diagnosed with a generalized anxiety disorder, there must be significant impairment in social, occupational, or other important areas of functioning, according to *DSM-5*.

An individual, such as Mike, also must have at least one of the following:

1. Restlessness or feeling keyed up or on edge
2. Being easily fatigued
3. Difficulty concentrating, or mind going blank
4. Irritability
5. Muscle tension
6. Sleep disturbance (difficulty falling or staying asleep, restlessness, unsatisfying sleep)

Students with an anxiety disorder often feel stressed about performance and evaluation by others. They also tend to be perfectionists, overly conforming, and have a tendency to constantly redo their work. Another marker is a strong need for approval, especially about their performance on a task.

In order for someone like Mike to be diagnosed with a generalized anxiety disorder, the impairment must be pervasive, distressing, long-lasting, and occur without a stimulus. Many individuals with this disorder show life-long persistent anxiety, and rates of complete remission are extremely low.

The Multidimensional Anxiety Scale for Children (MASC-2) is a 50-item questionnaire that can be completed by the individual or the parent. It captures a wide range of anxiety disorders in individuals aged 8–19 years old. For older individuals (17 through 80 years), the Beck Anxiety Inventory (BAI) is a 21-question self-report measure.

WHERE it is: Working memory and anxiety in the brain

Brain imaging studies on individuals with anxiety disorder have reported that the prefrontal cortex, the home of working memory, is affected by anxiety (Vytal et al., 2013). Anxiety induces a heavy cognitive load and impairs an individual's working memory, making it much less efficient. While the student may have the requisite working memory capacity to process a lesson on a new topic, when they experience anxiety their working memory capacity is minimized, making it much more effortful to pay attention to the lesson.

Here is an analogy to understand the effect of anxiety on learning. When you eat something extremely spicy, the capsaicin from the pepper binds to the pain receptors of your tongue and causes pain. Even when the capsaicin is removed, the heat and pain remain and other foods will not be as flavorful. A similar process occurs when you have an anxious thought in mind – it remains prominent in your PFC, diluting any new information that has to be processed and remembered.

Science Flash: Can the brain really change?

Researchers have found that chronic stress has an impact on the makeup of the human brain. Anxiety leads to an increased level of cortisol, the stress chemical of the brain, causing a chain reaction that leads to the production of fewer neurons and more of the nerve-covering myelin (Elzinga and Roelofs, 2005).

Cortisol levels in the brain affect the pathway between two major neurological structures: the hippocampus, the home of long-term memory, and the amygdala, the emotional control center. Anxiety disrupts the connection between the hippocampus and the amygdala and they do not communicate as well as they should. The stem cells created during stress produce a myelin sheath over the nerve cells in our prefrontal cortex (PFC), preventing new neurons from being formed that would otherwise improve the path from the hippocampus to the PFC, thus improving our memory. The take-home massage is that chronic stress will hamper the student's ability to use working memory and learn effectively.

WHY working memory is linked to anxiety

Anxiety disorders exert a two-fold impact on working memory: processing and storing information are both affected by anxiety. Anxiety causes invasive thoughts that trigger worry. Constant worry makes it more effortful to process new information efficiently, resulting in the student expending more effort and time completing a task. For instance, when writing an essay, a student with anxiety may take twice as long, as well as require twice the concentration and effort as their peers, because they are constantly worrying about whether their ideas are good enough or their content is perfect. The second aspect of working memory affected by anxiety is information storage. The invasive worrisome thoughts create an attentional bias, which prevents the student from processing new information and moving it to long-term memory.

Anxiety interferes with processing of **verbal** information in working memory. Think about a time when you were watching television or working on your computer, while someone was trying to talk to you. Your working memory was preoccupied with that task, so your attention to the person talking to you was compromised. As a result, you were unable to follow their conversation and had to ask them to repeat it. This is similar to how an anxious student feels when they are supposed to be listening to a lesson or classroom instructions. Their verbal working memory is consumed with worrisome thoughts so they are unable to process new information. In contrast, studies have shown that visual–spatial working memory is not affected by generalized or performance anxiety, because worrisome thoughts are managed by verbal and not visual–spatial resources (Castaneda et al., 2011). Anxiety also has an impact on academic performance, but this effect differs according to age group and by gender, as girls are more likely than boys to be diagnosed with an anxiety disorder.

Working memory and anxiety in young children

Young children with healthy anxiety levels can usually accomplish two tasks at once and can shift their attention from one task to another. Young students with high anxiety levels, however, are unable to manage multiple tasks efficiently, and struggle to shift their attention appropriately. A study with preschoolers confirmed that high levels of anxiety result in worse performance on verbal working memory tests compared to preschoolers with lower anxiety level. The children with high anxiety levels demonstrated greater difficulties in processing and recalling verbal information and also took longer to respond to the question when it was verbally demanding (Visu-Petra et al., 2011).

In the classroom, this is evident when the student is required to do two things at once, like practice drawing within lines and process the verbal information from their teacher during an activity. Think back to the Try It box – that activity represents how difficult it is to perform a task (mental math problem) while you are distracted by processing another piece of information (counting backwards).

Anxiety also impacts the acquisition of complex skills, like language. From a young age, students draw on their experiences to better understand the world. Part of this process is learning language to communicate and using working memory to match the words they hear with the words stored in their mental dictionary. Early childhood is an important age for language development, and anxiety can be particularly detrimental to this learning process. This obstruction is similar to being an adult in a foreign country where they do not know the language. Since they do not comprehend the words, it is hard for them to communicate.

Working memory and anxiety in middle childhood

Case Study: Daniel

Daniel, 16 years old, has been struggling all term to improve his test grades. This is his second time taking Algebra I and it is not likely that he will pass this time either. During test time, Daniel pulls his hair and shakes his knee up and down repeatedly, often mumbling to himself. His assignments are replete with eraser marks, scribbles, and doodles. He may get a few answers correct, but for the most part, he does not do well. He often skips class, and on the days he does show up, he keeps his head down and seldom communicates with the teacher or his peers.

The transition from middle school to high school can be very stressful for students but working memory can protect against this. Working memory acts as a buffer to help the student work through the stress and anxiety. In contrast, students like Daniel, who have low working memory, are especially vulnerable to the negative effects of anxiety. For instance, they would prepare for a high school geometry exam as if it was a college calculus exam. They are often very hard on themselves and expect the worst-case scenario. Without a good working memory, they have very little buffer against anxiety's disruptive effect and often underperform in exams despite over-preparing for them (Johnson and Gronlund, 2009).

But the effects of anxiety are not always negative. In adolescence, moderate levels of anxiety can be healthy and can motivate a student to perform well on exams to avoid negative feedback. Most of us can recall a time when we were nervous about an exam and spent countless hours studying to ensure we did well. Anxiety motivated us to work harder than we might otherwise. The combination of anxiety and good working memory can result in good grades, as we saw with Nicole at the beginning of this chapter. However, for the student with low working memory, the added burden of anxiety can be debilitating because they do not have sufficient working memory resources to manage the invasive worrisome thoughts (Owens et al., 2014).

Current Debate: Obsessive–Compulsive Disorder – the reality

Many people describe themselves as having obsessive–compulsive disorder (OCD) as a flippant way to characterize their idiosyncrasies, like 'Before I leave home for work I always get out of my car to make sure that my front door is locked; I guess it's just my OCD!' However, the reality is that OCD is a crippling anxiety disorder where intrusive thoughts are turned into a compulsion. Individuals with OCD are extremely ritualistic and perform strenuous and complicated activities to alleviate the anxiety caused by their own thoughts.

Imagine a young girl sitting at her class desk. She has her pen at the front of her desk, her papers stacked perfectly in the center of her desk, and her book placed neatly under her chair, the bindings all facing the same way. All around her, there are students whose pencils lie on the floor unsharpened, their papers crinkled and bunched together, and their books as foot-rests under their desks. Instead of remarking how neat and prepared for class this young girl is, we may think she has OCD. Yet, she does not have intrusive thoughts or compulsive actions due to extreme anxiety. Her neatness does not negatively affect her daily life, but instead it helps her accomplish tasks more efficiently.

Now, imagine a young boy who gets up from his desk to sharpen his pencil so often that he uses two pencils to write a one-page paper. When asked to stop sharpening his pencils, he becomes very distressed and complains, saying he cannot use a pencil that is not sharp. As a result of his preoccupation with his pencil, he takes longer to complete his paper and disrupts the class.

How does this boy compare to the neat young girl? The distinction lies with the anxiety underpinning their actions. The young girl's routines are not driven by a compulsive need for perfection; in contrast, the young boy's ritualistic behaviors are spurred on by an anxiety and worry about his ability to complete his assignment. OCD is a burden, causing an individual great difficulty in completing even simple activities, and flippant use of the term can show a disregard for those who suffer from this disorder.

Working memory and anxiety in adulthood

The detrimental effects of anxiety can persist in adulthood. For example, adults with high math anxiety tend to have lower working memory scores and perform worse in their math classes compared to their low-anxiety classmates (Ashcraft and Kirk, 2001). Adults who are not in college who have high anxiety levels also exhibit working memory difficulties, which can affect daily activities (Castaneda et al., 2011). Imagine that it is your first day at a new job in a big building. Using a map you printed out, you find your way to your office without any difficulty. The next day, you feel confident about your navigation skills and leave the map at home. However, when you get to the building, you realize that you have completely forgotten the location of your office. A week later, you still cannot find your office without your map. For the adult with an anxiety disorder, stressful situations like starting a new job are compounded by a poor working memory that is not sufficiently equipped to tackle simple tasks, like getting to their new office.

There is a key difference in how adults manage anxiety compared to young children or adolescents. When adults feel anxious, they typically avoid the activity that exacerbates their anxiety. For instance, college students with high levels of math anxiety will take fewer math classes than their less-anxious peers. In the short term, these students may feel good about this choice. However, in the long run they are doing a disservice to their working memory. Working memory thrives in a dynamic environment, and experiencing new things is key to developing, maintaining, and improving it. By avoiding such experiences, they are removing opportunities to develop their working memory.

HOW: Strategies to support working memory

Two types of strategies are discussed here: **general working memory strategies** that can be applied to students with anxiety disorders, and **specific working memory strategies** for students with generalized anxiety. While the general strategies below are tailored for those with anxiety, you can modify them as appropriate for other students in your classroom.

General strategies

Minimize distractions so working memory is not overwhelmed. Students with an anxiety disorder have poor working memory that is consumed with persistent worrisome thoughts. Distractions around them, such as posters and windows, can overload their working memory even more, making it difficult to learn new information and store it for later recall. Remove the distractions around them or move them to a different area of the classroom so they can learn more effectively.

Break down information to reduce working memory processing. The student with an anxiety disorder can be overwhelmed when being introduced to a new and complex topic. You can encourage the anxious student to be more receptive to learning by taking a complex topic and presenting it in smaller pieces. For instance, if you are teaching Newton's three laws of motion, try teaching each law on separate days to allow the student time to comprehend and process each law before they learn the next one.

Use learning tools and demonstrations to support working memory processing. Anxious students often have difficulty maintaining attention during a lesson. Keep them focused by using classroom demonstrations. For instance, the teacher can model Newton's first law, 'For every action there is an equal and opposite reaction', by asking two students to push their hands against one another's, creating equal pressure. This demonstration will maintain the student's attention, as well as encourage them to use working memory to process and remember the first law.

Repeat information intermittently to boost working memory. Repetition is important for storage of information because it keeps it in the forefront of working memory, allows for long-term storage, and supports future retrieval. Since a student with an anxiety disorder has poor working memory, they require more attention to move information into permanent storage. If you are teaching a student how to spell a word, say 'aquifer', first present a picture of an aquifer as the student repeats the letters. Repeated exposure to the spelling and associating the word with an image will support long-term storage of that word.

Shorten activities to reduce the working memory load. Taking breaks during learning activities is another way to avoid overwhelming an anxious student with too much information at one time. If the student is not given a break, they will 'zone out' and miss crucial information. After you present a new concept, stop and ask questions about the lesson so they can engage with the material. Breaks allow them to use their working memory to process new information at a steady pace and keep up with their classmates.

Use visual representation to support working memory. Students with anxiety disorders show poor verbal working memory scores compared to typical students. One way to bypass their weak verbal working memory and capitalize on their visual–spatial working memory is to use visual representation as part of the lesson. For example, ask the student to create a mental image to represent what they have just read or learned. Then ask them to explain their image.

Early years strategy. For younger students, ask them to draw a picture based on what they have heard or read. Then ask them to explain their picture, highlighting the 'big idea' in their picture, and discuss the supporting ideas. The eventual goal is to have students explain the lesson without creating a mental image or drawing a picture.

Specific strategies

Reduce social anxiety to support working memory processing. Social activities are very difficult for students with anxiety disorders because they are afraid of criticism from their peers. This can manifest itself in the classroom as an overly shy child who doesn't communicate much with his or his peers. To remedy this, a teacher can begin the class by having every student speak to the rest of the class. They can stand up at their desk and state one thing that they liked about yesterday's lesson.

On a smaller scale, the teacher can put the anxious student together with a group of students, and have each one introduce themselves. The goal is to make the student feel comfortable talking to their peers. By reducing the social anxiety, they can focus their working memory resources on the lesson instead of worrying about social relationships.

Use social prompts to support verbal working memory. Anxious students have poor verbal working memory and as a result find it hard to convey emotions, desires, or complete thoughts. Build their language skills by encouraging them to talk to their peers, and facilitate opportunities for them to do so. Have one-on-one conversations with them and pair them with a buddy to work together on some classroom activities.

Students with high levels of anxiety also tend to be fearful of expectations from their teachers and peers. Talk to the student about their concerns and dispel false expectations. By relieving their anxiety, you can remove the attentional bias of worry so they can engage their working memory to learn.

Early years strategy. Anxious young students often avoid interactions with their peers but this can hinder their language development. Take time to teach the young student basic conversational skills, like reciprocity and making eye contact in conversations so they feel less intimidated about joining in new conversations. When they start feeling comfortable talking to their peers, they can learn to process verbal cues more efficiently and will develop foundational language skills.

Set routines. Students with anxiety disorders do not like uncertainty or the resultant worry. Create a weekly lesson plan or syllabus and share it with them so they know what to expect. They will feel less anxious as a result and can use their working memory to focus on learning instead of being consumed with worrisome thoughts.

Create realistic expectations. Students with high levels of anxiety tend to display unhealthy levels of perfectionism. Furthermore, they have a sense of high, and often false, expectations. Offer the student individualized attention and candidly discuss your expectations of them. Provide them with structured goals so they can plan their work realistically. When you remove the veil of high expectations, the student will no longer feel nervous about disappointing you and can focus their working memory on meeting their learning goals instead.

Case Study: Ryan – social anxiety disorder

Ryan's behaviors in relation to *DSM-5*:

- Marked fear or anxiety about one or more social situations in which the individual is exposed to possible scrutiny by others
- The social situations almost always provoke fear or anxiety. In children, this causes crying, tantrums, freezing, clinging, shrinking, or failing to speak in social situations
- The social situations are avoided or endured with intense fear or anxiety
- The fear, anxiety, or avoidance is persistent, typically lasting for 6 months or more

For the past year, Ryan, 8 years old, had been acting out when his mother dropped him off for school. Some weeks were worse than others. One week, he threw a tantrum every time his mother dropped him off; the next week, he threw only two morning tantrums. On his bad mornings he would cling to his mother's leg, yelling at her not to leave him.

He avoided talking to any of his classmates. When he was put into a group, he was silent and would not partake in group activities. He also refused to talk to any of the adults at the school, other than his classroom teacher. He secluded himself in other settings, like lunch and recess. In recess, he would sit by himself on a swing, away from the other children. During lunch, even when he was surrounded by his peers, he kept his head down and didn't say a word. He often asked me to let him eat lunch in the classroom by himself.

(Continued)

(Continued)

Since Ryan was too shy to talk to anyone, he was unable to learn conversational rules and found it difficult to communicate simple emotions. For example, when I asked him what was wrong when he seemed upset, he looked at me blankly. When I repeated the question, he said, 'I don't know'. His verbal comprehension was also so poor that it was difficult for him to follow simple instructions, like 'Go to the library and pick up a dictionary for the class'. He often became flustered and returned to class empty-handed.

Strategies

- Break down information to reduce working memory processing

I wanted to encourage Ryan's involvement in the class by giving him simple tasks to accomplish, like collect a book from the library. I wrote down each step so he could keep track of his place: (1) walk to the library; (2) find a librarian; (3) ask for a dictionary; (4) walk back to class. These step-by-step instructions reduced the load on his working memory and allowed him to complete the task with very little anxiety. Eventually, I could just write down what I needed from the library and he was able to go there and come back with the correct book.

- Reduce social anxiety to support working memory processing

When Ryan was required to work in group projects, I placed him with the same group of students every time. I first asked everyone in the group to introduce themselves and share their favorite animal. When it came to Ryan's turn, I sat next to him and helped him talk to his group members, prompting him to say more when necessary. Once he felt more comfortable with his group members, I left them to begin the assignment. He seemed less anxious about contributing to the assignment and was able to use his working memory to process the task without further prompting.

- Use social prompts to support verbal working memory

After class I spent time talking to Ryan to ask him about his day. When he struggled to answer my questions, I prompted him by asking, 'How was your day?' If he still seemed confused, I asked, 'Did you have a good day? A bad day?' I gave him specific prompts to allow him to choose an appropriate response and associate it with a feeling. The next time I asked him a similar question, he already knew the options and could pull from his experience to respond.

Case Study: Bianca – generalized anxiety disorder

Bianca's behaviors in relation to *DSM-5*:

- The individual finds it difficult to control the worry
- Excessive anxiety and worry (apprehensive expectation), occurring more days than not for at least 6 months, about an event or activities (such as work or school performance)
- Being easily fatigued
- Irritability
- Sleep disturbance (difficulty falling or staying asleep, restlessness, unsatisfying sleep)

Bianca, 18 years old, is a trumpet player in the marching band at her high school. During band class she falls asleep at the back of the room. When her class practices marching outside on the field, she rarely has the energy to get out and join them for more than a few minutes. When the band director speaks to her about her behavior, she becomes very upset and storms away. Even when her friends confront her, she yells at them and storms away.

In an attempt to get her more involved, the band director gave her a solo part in the upcoming marching show. Bianca refused to play it and gave it to one of her fellow trumpet players instead. She also would not show up to play at the weekly half-time show at their high school football game. She says that she does not like to play in front of the crowd. She also leaves the game shortly after arriving because she is too tired to stay and play with the band in the bleachers (spectator stands) for the remainder of the game.

Strategies

- Reduce stress load to free up working memory processing

Bianca was a good trumpet player but she was always very stressed about performing in front of people. The band director decided to give her music that didn't stand out in the arrangement and allowed her to blend in with the rest of the band. When she didn't feel like she was the focus of attention, she became less anxious about making mistakes. She soon took a more active part in playing with the band and became more confident in her trumpet playing ability.

(Continued)

(Continued)

- Shorten activities to reduce the working memory load

Bianca complained a lot about being tired. Her fatigue carried over to her playing and marching ability and she was unable to engage her working memory to memorize marching steps or pieces of music. To overcome this issue, the band director allowed her to take breaks during marching practice. Unlike other students, who were required to stand, Bianca was allowed to sit on the ground until she needed to play again. These rests allowed her to be more involved when it was her group's turn to march or play a part of a song. As a result, she was better able to retain information, like the musical notes or steps in the marching arrangement.

- Use social prompts to support verbal working memory

When Bianca struggled to remember marching arrangements or music notes this frustrated her and she would quit in the middle of practice. The band director began allowing her to come in during lunch or after school to practice. Together, they went over the music, note by note, piece by piece. They also went over the marching steps so she could perform her part with ease. By giving her individualized attention, the band director helped her automatize both the notes she had to play and the marching steps. This process greatly reduced her performance anxiety and in a few short weeks she was able to confidently play all of her music from memory, as well as march along with the band with no mistakes.

Summary

1. **Core deficit**: Students with anxiety disorders are bombarded with worrisome thoughts. The worry can be so invasive that they keep focusing on negative reoccurring thoughts, a phenomenon referred to as 'attentional bias'.
2. **Working memory profile**: Impairments in verbal working memory are very common in young students with anxiety disorders. As these students grow, their working memory impairment persists, often until adulthood.
3. **Strategies**: Reducing the stress load is key to allowing working memory to function efficiently. Breaking down information and tasks, as well as developing tools to overcome stress, are important strategies to support the student with an anxiety disorder to function fully in a classroom or social setting.

References and further reading

Ashcraft, M.H. and Kirk, E.P. (2001) The relationship among working memory, math anxiety, and performance. *Journal of Experimental Psychology*, 130(2): 224–37.

Castaneda, A.E., Suvisaan, J., Marttuen, M., Perälä, J., Saarni, S.I., Aalto-Setälää, T., Lönnqvista, J., and Tuulio-Henriksson, A. (2011) Cognitive functioning in a population-based sample of young adults with anxiety disorders. *European Psychiatry*, 26(6): 346–53.

Elzinga, B.M. and Roelofs, K. (2005) Cortisol-induced impairments of working memory require acute sympathetic activation. *Behavioral Neuroscience*, 119 (1): 98–103.

Johnson, D.R. and Gronlund, S.D. (2009) Individuals with lower working memory capacity are particularly vulnerable to anxiety's disruptive effect on performance. *Anxiety, Stress & Coping*, 22(2): 201–13.

Lupien, S.J., McEwen, B.S., Gunnar, M.R., and Heim, C. (2009) Effects of stress throughout the lifespan on the brain, behaviour and cognition. *Nature Reviews Neuroscience*, 10(6): 434–45.

Owens, M., Stevenson, J., Hadwin, J.A., and Norgate, R. (2014) When does anxiety help or hinder cognitive test performance? The role of working memory capacity. *British Journal of Psychology*, 105: 92–101.

Visu-Petra, L., Cheie, L., Benga, O., and Alloway, T.P. (2011) Effects of anxiety on memory storage and updating in young children. *International Journal of Behavior Development*, 35(1): 38–47.

Vytal, K.E., Cornwell, B.R., Letkiewicz, A.M., Arkin, N.E., and Grillon, C. (2013) The complex interaction between anxiety and cognition: insight from spatial and verbal working memory. *Frontiers in Human Neuroscience*, 7: 1–11.

CHAPTER 9

STUDENT STRATEGIES AND TRAINING

This chapter looks at:

- Ways to develop student-centered learning.
- Ways to encourage the student to be more independent in their learning.
- Evidence for the efficacy of working memory training.

One of the hardest things about having a learning disorder is the label itself, because it can lead to a sense of 'learned helplessness' in the student. Jim, now a straight-A college student, recounts his grade-school years when he was diagnosed with ADHD. Like most boys his age, he was an active student, but he was loud, would play roughly with his peers, and had trouble focusing during lessons. On his first day back to class after being diagnosed with ADHD, he was walking around and tossing paper balls around the classroom, instead of sitting down quietly. However, the teacher overlooked his unruly behavior because she knew he was diagnosed with ADHD. His performance in class also worsened. Jim used his diagnosis of ADHD as a crutch and often gave up on his homework after only a few problems, but again, the teacher excused him.

When Jim started college, he realized that his diagnosis did not have to define him and he became more invested in his learning. He soon began doing well in his classes and was often used as a role model for his peers.

Jim, and students like him, can feel a sense of powerlessness when it comes to their learning and this can affect their self-esteem. A large-scale study of more than 3000 students found that students with working memory deficits had a low sense of *personal power*, or their sense of their ability to influence their surroundings. They are aware of their struggles in the classroom and lose confidence as a result. These students are often emotionally fragile, and benefit from tools to build up their confidence (Alloway et al., 2009).

While much of this book is about how teachers can support their students, this chapter is about how students can support themselves. By being responsible for their own successes, students can gain a measure of self-belief that empowers them to achieve improved outcomes. When they discover that their learning disability does not have to define them or their performance, you may find that they need increasingly less support to achieve improved results. This chapter discusses tools that facilitate self-empowered learning.

Meta-awareness

Meta-awareness is being aware of why you are doing what you are doing. It means intentionally employing an approach that is appropriate for the task at hand. Sometimes for students, things just click and they are in the 'learning zone': they take notes well, they understand the math problems, and they ace the spelling test. Sometimes, though, nothing seems to work. By being aware of the big picture, by being 'meta'-aware, the student can step out of the immediate specifics of their learning context and get a bird's-eye view of when things work well and when they don't. By being meta-aware of the process when learning went smoothly, students can repeat it, and spend more time *in* the learning zone than outside it.

Susan, a special needs teacher in London, described the joy she felt when after weeks of teaching her student Max how to diagram sentences he finally understood it. She went home that Friday afternoon so pleased at the student's progress. Imagine her disappointment on Monday morning when she saw him making the same errors again. When she asked him why he did it correctly on Friday but was struggling again on Monday, he just shrugged his shoulders.

Students can be oblivious to the steps they took to get to the correct answer, but there are clear prompts that teachers like Susan can use to enable students like Max to repeat their success.

- **Step 1: WHAT did you do?** When asked this question, a student may say, 'I don't know' or 'I just did it'. Encourage them – ask them what strategy they used to complete the task successfully. If a student who usually struggles at mental math is suddenly able to calculate '13 + 17' correctly, prompt them to put into words how they arrived at the answer. They may say something like 'I knew 10 plus 10 equals 20, and 3 plus 7 equals 10, and then I just added it all up.' Now, you can help them recognize why that works, and help them solve other problems in a similar manner, by adding the tens place first, followed by the ones.
- **Step 2: WHY did you do that?** When learning spelling words, they may unconsciously sing the letters. This is a common phenomenon, possibly related to students first learning the alphabet in a song. If you see a student using this strategy successfully, ask them why they do it. They may give an answer like: 'It is easier for me to remember things when I sing.' Encourage them to articulate why they chose a particular strategy.
- **Step 3: WHEN can you use it again?** Students with poor working memory often view strategies as a one-off activity and don't consider applying them to different problems. Although the connection between their strategy use and the lesson may become clearer to them, they may still struggle to generate examples of when they can apply it again. Continuing the example from Step 2, for many students music is more memorable than speech. Now that they know they were using music because it helped them remember their spelling, ask them to come up with other situations in which they could use their newly recognized strategy. They may want to see how many things they can sing, like history (a song about the order of kings and queens), math (times tables), and science (taxonomic rank).
- **Step 4: HOW will it help you?** This is an important step. Some strategies are better than others. In fact, the strategies they are using may even get in the way of them doing something successfully. For example, Gemma used to break down numbers into tens when adding anything over 20, such that '74 + 57' would look something like '74 + 10 + 10 + 10 + 10 + 10 + 7'. The problem is that this strategy was time-consuming and required her working memory to keep track of how many tens she had added, and how many were left to add. When Gemma was asked how this strategy was helpful, she realized on her own that she would be better off memorizing addition of tens, like '80 + 40' up to 200, and then adding the ones place. Now Gemma is much better at mental addition.

Encoding: getting the information in

'Encoding' is the term psychologists use to describe how we take information we don't know and change it into something that can be remembered easily. One of the best ways to encode information – to get information into our head – is to make it meaningful by mapping it on to something that is already in there. Let's take the fact that Harald Fairhair was the first king of Norway. Because this piece of information is so far removed from our historical identity, it is arbitrary and very hard to remember on its own. If we had to remember this information for a test, most of us would struggle to recall it. However, encoding will allow us to remember arbitrary information.

Create a connection with long-term memory

The first step to remembering that Harald Fairhair was the first king of Norway is to create a connection with long-term memory. Long-term memory is a huge store of information that refers to the stored knowledge we have about the world. This includes our mental dictionary of language, such as our understanding of meaning and how words relate to each other. For example, we know that our pet dog is a mammal and belongs to the category of animals. Think of long-term memory like a web or a map of interconnected relationships. By encouraging your students to draw on this rich resource, they can come up with creative and fun ways to support their working memory.

Let's go back to Harald. We draw on our long-term memory to get this fact in our head by making up a story. We need to remember that Harald was the first king in Norway, and part of his name was Fairhair. A student may use their semantic memory to construct a fair (fair) in their mind, where they see a hairy (hair) king (king) being announced by a herald (Harald). The king comes first (first) in a pie-eating contest. Of course this story is bizarre, even weird, but that makes it easier to remember because it sticks out in the mind.

Category cues

Another way to encode is to use category cues to help students remember. Imagine that you are teaching them new vocabulary words: *fedora*, *tuxedo, trousers, chaise longue, chandelier, vanity*. Ask the students to group the items that belong together and then give them category headings to help them retrieve this information. Studies have found that when we have category cues, like 'clothes' and 'furniture' for the example above, we are twice as likely to remember all the words associated with the category. You can try this with any group of items like colors or eating utensils (like fork, spoon, and knife). When teaching new vocabulary or spelling words, group them according to categories.

Rule of threes (for longer texts)

Ask students to come up with three main points when they read a text. Have them identify the main idea and two supporting points. This process can help them both recognize the important information in the text and exclude less significant information in the text. The effort they spend processing the information will make it more 'sticky' in their mind.

Talk aloud

Ask the students to discuss what they read in groups. Studies have found that when students talk about what they have read, they remember more information than if they just read a list of summary points.

Retrieval: getting the information out

Now that the student has the information in their head, they need to retrieve it. This requires working memory to search through information in long-term memory and find the right answer to put down on paper.

Test yourself instead of re-studying material

To prepare for a test, most students reread the material with the hope that they will remember it. However, research shows that the best way to prepare for a test is to test yourself. One study showed that participants remembered 50% more information when they tested themselves compared to just reading.

Hypothetical scenarios

If you want students to have a deeper understanding of the material, encourage them to use their working memory to process what they have committed to long-term memory. Hypothetical scenarios are an excellent way of doing this because they require the use of working memory to imagine the information in a new context. For example, if you are teaching them about Thomas Jefferson, ask them to pretend that they are Thomas Jefferson and they have traveled through time to the present day. Now they have to use Jefferson's political skills to resolve a disagreement between two groups on whether chocolate or vanilla is the best flavor of ice cream. Ask them how Jefferson would approach this dilemma. By considering how Jefferson would adjust to the present day, and what he would do, they have to work with what they already know about Jefferson and apply it in interesting ways.

Create a bridge

A great way to recall arbitrary information is to create a bridge between new information and long-term knowledge. Dominic O'Brien is the eight-time winner of the World Memory Championships and holds many titles in the Guinness Book of World Records. One of his amazing feats is to memorize 54 decks of playing cards in just a few hours. When working with O'Brien at the UK Schools Memory Championship, Tracy was able to watch him use a bridge with 15- and 16-year-olds.

He first gives them a list of arbitrary words to remember: *bomb, helium, light, beryl, coal*. Most of the students struggle to remember all the words, and by lunchtime, only a handful can still recite just three words from the list. O'Brien tells them the following story:

> You are asleep in your bed one night when you hear a loud explosion. It sounds like a bomb. Before you can do anything, you spot a helium balloon in the sky shining a bright light on the ground. You think they are looking for the perpetrator. The light seems to be moving towards your room but instead it stops and shines on your neighbor Beryl's house. You start to worry that more bombs will start going off so you make your way out of the house and into the garden. Someone has left a large bag of coal in the middle of the walkway and you trip over it in the dark.

The story goes on and you can imagine that the students are drawn into it. O'Brien then reveals that the words in the list provide a clue to the first few elements in the Periodic Table: bomb (hydrogen), helium (helium), light (lithium), Beryl (beryllium), coal (carbon). Now the students can easily remember them simply by thinking about the story. To their amazement, they find that by the end of the day, they are able to recall the 15 words in the correct order and can even recite them backwards.

Daily habits

There are small tweaks that the student can do in their daily life that can make a big impact on their learning.

Diet

One of the most important things that students have control over is what they put in their mouth: what they eat is how they think. This is because our brains are built on what passes our lips.

Trans fats vs. omega-3. A student who is constantly eating foods high in 'junk' fats, like trans fats, has a hard time performing in school. A student who primarily eats good fats, like omega-3, has a brain ready for work (Northstone et al., 2011).

Trans fats are bad for brains in part because of their molecular shape and rigidity. You can think of trans fats like a crowbar: it is 'stiff' and straight. You can compare this to an omega-3 fat, which is comparatively flexible, and has the shape of a coiled spring: it is 'bendy'. The neurons that fill your brain are made up of the fats that you eat. Your body much prefers making neurons built with flexible fats like omega-3 fats, but if you eat a lot of trans fats, it will be forced to build the neurons with what it has to hand.

The brain at work is like a mini electrical storm of thoughts that are passed between parts of the brain (like the prefrontal cortex, the home of working memory) and through the neurons that comprise them. As electrical signals travel between neurons, they must pass through the tiny tunnels in the cell walls. A neuron made up of bendy fat has bendy tunnels that quickly change shape to accommodate the electrical signal. On the other hand, a tunnel made up of stiff fat has a much harder time accommodating the signal. If you have ever wondered why binging on junk food makes it much harder to think, you now know that bad fats play a role in damaging your neurons.

Flavonoids. Foods that include flavonoids are great for working memory. Flavonoids are powerful anti-oxidants found in plant-based foods. They improve circulation in the brain, allowing students to get blood to the parts of the brain where it is needed most; they modulate neuroinflammation that can damage neurons and they help regenerate neurons. Foods rich in flavonoids include berries (blueberries, blackberries, and raspberries are particularly good), dark chocolate (70% or higher cocoa), plums, spinach, and kale. A study found that flavonoids improve working memory (Macready et al., 2009), so encourage parents to include a little cup of berries and a square of dark chocolate for a brain boost during snack time.

Drink your milk! Milk doesn't just do the body good, it does the brain good as well. Milk and milk products, like yoghurt and cheese, are great for working memory in moderate amounts. Research shows that dairy consumption can have a beneficial effect on cognition in young adults and the elderly (Crichton et al., 2012), though more studies are needed to verify if children receive the same cognitive benefits. On the other hand, milk is full of beneficial components like calcium and protein that growing students need.

Finding balance. Teachers should encourage parents to build their child's brain with things that are good for it. The key is finding the right balance. If students eat things that are good for their cognition, you will find they perform better in class than if they hadn't. Of course, life would be pretty boring without the occasional splurge. A few slices of pizza, a small bag of chips (crisps), a doughnut, or a hamburger aren't going to ruin a child's working memory, and can even be used as a motivational reward for a good effort in school. However, a diet primarily composed of such foods will have a negative impact. Knowledge of how certain foods can boost (and hinder) school performance can empower parents and students to make better choices and find the balance.

Sleep

The more time a child spends in bed, the better it is for their working memory. Sleep is a powerful support for working memory (Whitney and Rosen, 2012). Unfortunately, in today's hyper-connected world where children have access to tablets, TVs, phones, video games, entertainment, and time online, it is commonplace for many children's rooms to be lit by a screen's bluish glow late into the night. This can considerably reduce the amount of sleep. When children go without adequate sleep, they struggle academically because key brain areas, including math and language areas, shut down. Though the prefrontal cortex, the home of working memory, doesn't stop, it is forced to step in and pick up the slack for those areas that aren't working. This puts it in the position of doing double duty.

Imagine you were supposed to play the title role in *Hamlet*, but none of the other actors bothered to show up because they had spent the night before at a cast party. Of course, the show must go on because you can't cancel a play for tired actors any more than you can skip a test because you didn't study. So instead of acting only your own role, you now have to play Hamlet, Ophelia, your mother, and the illegitimate king. You may be a great Hamlet – in fact, you may be as good as Richard Burton – but because you are now tasked with acting so many different roles, the play is going to flop. If students want to get the best out of their working memory, they need to let their brains get a good rest so that every actor can perform their roles appropriately. Here are the approximate sleep needs for students by grade:

- Preschoolers to kindergarten (age 4–6): 12 hours
- First grade to junior high (age 7–13): Fewer than 10 hours
- High school (age 14–18): 9 hours

The importance of sleep cannot be stressed enough, and as a teacher you may want to give your class some 'sleep homework' where they are encouraged to get sleep, just like an assignment, so that their whole brain shows up to class.

Science Flash: Technology in the classroom

Is technology hurting our working memory? From our ever-increasing reliance on word processing to help us improve grammar, to smart-phones to remind us of appointments, speed-dial so we don't have to remember phone numbers, and a universe of information available at the click of a mouse, is there a trade-off? Is social media, like Facebook, reducing our ability to engage our working memory in daily life? In fact, the opposite may be true: technology can dramatically improve our working memory.

Facebook is one of the most popular social networking sites, with more than 300 million active users. Apart from the novelty of connecting with people you haven't seen since you were 5 years old (for better or for worse!), it can also promote a sense of social connectedness. Those who are cut off from others often become isolated and may miss out on many benefits within education and employment. Studies on elderly populations found that those who spent more time meeting up with friends or talking on the phone experienced less memory loss than their more isolated peers.

Technology is advancing quickly and more and more students use social networking sites. But what impact does this have on education and can this boost working memory? These questions were examined in a study with a group of high-schoolers (age 15–17; Alloway, Horton, et al., 2013). They filled in a questionnaire about how long they spent using social networking sites, such as Facebook, and the study also measured their IQ, working memory, and academic attainment (language and math).

The study found that high-schoolers who used Facebook more regularly (once a day) had better working memory, as well as higher language scores. One explanation for the better working memory scores could be because using Facebook involves working memory. For example, when you log into Facebook, you must first take in the information from the news feed, process it in order to prioritize it and determine what is relevant to you and what isn't, and finally plan an action based on this information. Students may be getting a 'mini working memory workout' whenever they engage in this process. This is good news for schools that are integrating social networking sites into their programs.

Working memory training

This book provides strategies to support working memory in the classroom – a scaffold for learning. But one question that always comes up at presentations to schools or at educational conferences is whether we can increase the size of our working memory. For a long time, psychologists thought that we were stuck with our working memory size and couldn't change it. However, exciting cutting-edge research suggests that we can train our brain and improve working memory.

In response to this, there has been a surge of brain-training products in the last 5–10 years and some of these have found their way into schools. Based on research, here are three key things to look for when evaluating the programs and the research behind them.

1. **Control group.** A control group offers a comparison to make sure that the training program is not just working because the student is doing something different. Some studies use a control group who don't do *anything*. While this is a good start, an ideal control group is a group of people who are doing *something* – something different from the training program (such as reading or playing a different computer game). Look for research findings that include an active control group to compare with the training group.
2. **Transfer effects.** This refers to whether the program improves anything other than getting better at the game itself. Practicing one thing will naturally make you better at it. This is known as a *practice effect*. But can the benefits of a brain training program transfer to real-world activities? In other words, can you get better at something other than the training game?

3. **Maintenance.** How long do the results last? It is important to consider whether the training benefits will last beyond the training period. Not all research studies include a follow-up from the training program so you may not know whether the benefits of the training program last more than a day or a week.

How do different programs stand up against these criteria? Here is a brief overview of some of the programs that are commonly used in schools around the world.

Computer games for brain training

Computer games that are targeted to improve brain functioning have received a lot of attention. While they may be enjoyable, is there any evidence that they actually improve learning? One study compared the benefits of playing a brain training program by Nintendo with paper-and-pencil puzzles in school children. The researchers found that the brain training program provided no more benefit compared to the paper-and-pencil puzzles. In a follow-up study, the researchers found that first- and second-graders' (average age was 10 years) working memory scores did not improve despite playing the computer game for 6 week (Lorant-Royer et al., 2008, 2010). There was **no transfer effect**.

Working memory training programs

There are two types of working memory training programs: those that are narrow in scope and those that are broad in scope. Let's use an example from an exercise to understand the difference between these two programs. A narrow-scope program targets just one area – like doing bicep curls to improve the muscle tone in your arms. In contrast, a broad-scope program has a wider application – like running for your general cardiovascular health.

Narrow-scope training. These working memory training programs are very similar to a working memory test. For example, they require the student to remember numbers in backwards order or the location of dots in backwards order. Will this type of narrow-scope training boost working memory? The research findings to date suggest some students do achieve higher working memory scores but it may be attributed to a practice effect. When a student repeats numbers in backwards order for several weeks, they will naturally perform better on a test where they have to remember numbers in backwards order. Indeed, the research on some of these programs indicates that there is **no transfer effect** for grades, as these did not immediately improve after such training. So a program that simply encourages the student to 'train for the test' may not yield lasting benefits for learning.

Broad-scope working memory training. These programs train working memory in the context of key learning skills. One published study (Alloway, 2012) recruited students with learning difficulties, half of whom played *Jungle Memory*™, which is a working memory training program developed by Ross, while the **active control group** received targeted educational support. The students' memory, IQ, and academic attainment were measured at the beginning of the study and the students in both groups performed on a similar level in these cognitive tests. This is important because it means that any improvement the students subsequently make is the result of the training and not because they started at different levels.

Figure 9.1 shows the difference in scores between the pre- and post-testing time between the control and training groups. Scores below 0 (marked by the line) indicate that the group performed worse when tested 8 weeks later. Scores above 0 indicate improvements that the group made after 8 weeks.

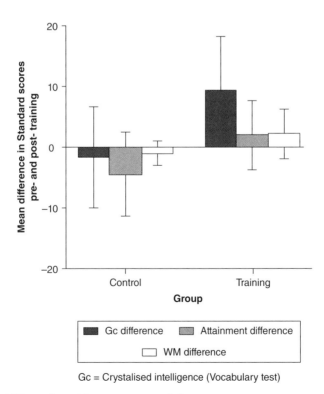

Gc = Crystalised intelligence (Vocabulary test)

Figure 9.1   Effect of working memory training

The results are dramatic. The active control group did not perform much better without working memory training. In contrast, the training group demonstrated a clear gain not only in working memory tasks, but crucially in learning outcomes as well. For example, in a language-based test, their scores increased by almost 10 standard score points. Are these score increases meaningful? Yes – they represent the difference between the grades of C and B, or between B and A – after just 8 weeks of training. This indicates a **transfer effect** of the training to standardized tests of attainment.

The improvements in learning outcomes after working memory training can be compared with a phenomenon in IQ known as the *Flynn effect*, which is the reported steady increase in IQ scores over the last 50 years. The increase in IQ scores, however, is much more modest: on average, it is 3 points per decade. Compare the IQ score rise with the increase reported here after just 8 weeks of working memory training–the same increase in math (3 points) and a much larger rise in spelling (8 points).

One question is whether students would have demonstrated such improvements without working memory training. The answer can be found in a previous study (Alloway, 2009) that tracked 8- to 10-year-olds with learning difficulties over a 2-year period. All of these students were receiving targeted educational support during this time. Yet when their academic skills were tested at the end of the 2-year period, they remained in the bottom 10th percentile compared with their same-aged peers. This finding suggests that students with poor working memory will not 'catch up' with their peers, without the right working memory support and training.

A further published study of almost 100 students found that the benefits of *Jungle Memory* training persisted when students were tested 8 months later (Alloway, Bibile, et al., 2013). The study also included an **active control group**. The findings demonstrated that students who trained regularly with *Jungle Memory* improved their working memory scores by five times more than those who trained only once a week. Their language and math scores also improved considerably, confirming a **transfer effect**. *Jungle Memory* was demonstrated to improve not just working memory, but more importantly, grades as well.

But the most exciting news came 8 months later: when these same students we retested and all the improvements they had achieved had been maintained – *even though none of them had been training during that period*. This **maintenance effect** suggests that these students had made lasting gains to their working memory.

Pilot trials run in association with Dyslexia Scotland also demonstrated that adults with dyslexia made significant gains in working memory and

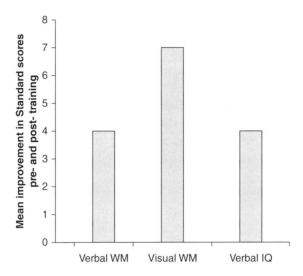

Figure 9.2 Effect of working memory training with adults

verbal IQ scores after training with *Jungle Memory*. Their improvements are shown in Figure 9.2, where the higher the number, the greater the improvements (using standard scores). There are more trials under way, but the evidence so far is showing that the right working memory training can offer improvements that last.

Conclusion

Let's end this book with Jasmine, a sweet 10-year-old, whom one of the authors encountered when working in the UK. Like any young girl, she desperately wanted to fit in, but she couldn't keep up with her classmates because she wasn't able to remember the teacher's instructions or even remember which books she was supposed to be using in class. 'Life was hard. I couldn't do what the teacher said. I just felt like I was terrible,' Jasmine said in a TV interview with a leading UK network. In that same interview, Jasmine's mother, Emma, said, 'School was always about Jasmine being made to feel stupid.' Some evenings, her mother found her crying alone in her room because she couldn't remember what she was supposed to do. Simple tasks like tidying up and organizing her books for school the next day seemed to overwhelm her.

A recent assessment by the school psychologist had identified Jasmine as in the bottom percentile for working memory. Armed with this information, her mother looked for solutions and came across *Jungle Memory*.

Jasmine used the program over the summer and when she returned to school in September, her teacher was amazed. She said that Jasmine was a completely different student and you wouldn't know that she had learning difficulties. Jasmine no longer needed extra help in the classroom and her grades improved.

Emma noticed a big improvement at home as well. Jasmine could now accomplish what she needed to do without feeling frustrated. When the school psychologist retested Jasmine, her IQ had increased to the top 10% for her age and her working memory had improved to average levels.

Emma says:

> I am thrilled at Jasmine's meteoric improvements and can only attribute them to *Jungle Memory*. Jasmine continues to go from strength to strength with her memory skills. She received a memory certificate in school last week, which I thought would make you smile. She's certainly never received any kind of accolade for her memory skills before!

Jasmine herself says it best: 'I'm better at remembering, better at times tables, and my teacher was like, "Wow! You've learned a lot!"'

The wonderful news is that Jasmine's story is not unique. So many educators and parents report that working memory and grades improve after receiving working memory support. We are excited by this, because it offers real hope to the struggling student. Armed with targeted strategies and the right kind of working memory training, we can make a difference in our students' lives.

Summary

1. Developing meta-awareness teaches students how to use the tools (strategies) in their cognitive toolbox and promotes self-empowered learners.
2. Long-term memory is a huge store of information and can be used as an anchor when learning new information.
3. Small changes in daily habits, like diet and sleep, can make a big impact in working memory performance.
4. Some working memory training programs, like *Jungle Memory*, have been shown to increase working memory, IQ, and grades, with lasting effects.

References and further reading

Alloway, T.P., Gathercole, S.E., Kirkwood, H.J. and Elliott, J.E. (2009) The cognitive and behavioural characteristics with low working menory. *Child Development*, 80, 606–21.

Alloway, T.P. (2012) Can interactive working memory training improving learning? *Journal of Interactive Learning Research*, 23: 1–11.

Alloway, T.P. and Alloway, R.G. (2012) The impact of engagement with social networking sites (SNSs) on cognitive skills. *Computers and Human Behavior*, 28: 1748–54.

Alloway, T.P., Bibile, V., and Lau, G. (2013) Computerized working memory training: can it lead to gains in cognitive skills in students? *Computers & Human Behavior*, 29: 632–8.

Alloway, T.P., Horton, J., Alloway, R.G., and Dawson, C. (2013) The impact of technology and social networking on working memory. *Computers & Education*, 63: 10–16.

Alloway, T.P. (2009) Working memory, but not IQ, predicts subsequent learning in children with learning difficulties. *European Journal of Psychological Assessment*, 25, 92–8.

Crichton, G.E., Elias, M., Dore, G., and Robbins, M. (2012) Relation between dairy food intake and cognitive function: the Maine–Syracuse Longitudinal Study. *International Dairy Journal*, 22: 15–23.

Francis, S.T., Head, K., Morris, P.G., and Macdonald, I.A. (2006) The effect of flavanol-rich cocoa on the fMRI response to a cognitive task in healthy young people. *Journal of Cardiovascular Pharmacology*, 47: S215–S220.

Jungle Memory™ (www.junglememory.com)

Lorant-Royer, S., Spiess, V., Goncalves, J., and Lieury, A. (2008) Programmes d'entraînement cérébral et performances cognitives : efficacité ou marketing? De la gym-cerveau au programme du Dr Kawashima. *Bulletin de Psychologie*, 61: 531–49.

Lorant-Royer, S., Munch, C., Mesclé, H., and Lieury, A. (2010) Kawashima vs 'Super Mario'! Should a game be serious in order to stimulate cognitive aptitudes? *European Review of Applied Psychology*, 60: 221–32.

Macready, A., Kennedy, O., Ellis, J., Williams, C., Spencer, J., and Butler, L. (2009) Flavonoids and cognitive function: a review of human randomized controlled trial studies and recommendations for future studies. *Genes & Nutrition*, 4: 227–42.

Narendran, R., Frankle, W., Mason., N., Muldoon, M., and Moghaddam, B. (2012) Improved working memory but no effect on striatal vesicular monoamine transporter type 2 after omega-3 polyunsaturated fatty acid supplementation. *PLOS ONE* 7: e46832.

Northstone, K., Joinson, C., Emmett, P., Ness, A., and Paus, T. (2011) Are dietary patterns in childhood associated with IQ at 8 years of age? A population-based cohort study. *Journal of Epidemiology and Community Health*, 66(7): 624–8.

O'Brien, D. (2009) *Learn to Remember*. London: Duncan Baird.

Pilcher, J. and Huffcutt, A. (1996) Effects of sleep deprivation on performance: a meta analysis. *Sleep*, 19: 318–26.

Smith, M., Rigby, L., Van Eekelen, A., and Foster, J. (2011) Glucose enhancement of human memory: a comprehensive research review of the glucose memory facilitation effect. *Neuroscience and Biobehavioral Reviews*, 35: 770–83.

Steenari, M.R., Vuontela, V., Paavonen, E.J., Carlson, S., Fjallberg, M., and Aronen, E. (2003) Working memory and sleep in 6- to 13-year-old schoolchildren. *Journal of the American Academy of Child and Adolescent Psychiatry*, 42: 85–92.

Whitney, P. and Rosen, P. (2012) Sleep deprivation and performance: the role of working memory, in T.P. Alloway and R.G. Alloway (eds), *Working Memory: The Connected Intelligence*. New York: Psychology Press.

EPILOGUE: A SCHOOL-BASED PROGRAM TO SUPPORT WORKING MEMORY AND LEARNING

Kim Grant

When I was asked to write a few pages about my experience of identifying and supporting students with working memory problems I was both excited and apprehensive. I was excited because I very much wanted to share what we have been doing in my school district. However, I was also concerned about how to convey my professional passion. I decided the best course of action was to share my experience and hope that it would benefit teachers and psychologists in their own working memory journeys.

My working memory journey

I stumbled on working memory quite unexpectedly when working as a school psychologist. When conducting learning disability evaluations, I started noticing that many of the students referred for reading and math evaluations also had difficulty retaining information in the classroom. When I tested them, I often found a weakness in working memory. I wondered: Is there a relationship between their low academic achievement and their working memory problems? I did not have an answer, so I began to investigate. My search led me to Dr Tracy Alloway and her colleagues'

Kimberly Phillips Grant, EdS, NCSP, is a school psychologist in a US Midwestern suburban school district.

research, as well as research by other working memory leaders such as Dr Milton Dehn and Dr Torkel Klingberg. My review of their research and books enabled me to develop a better understanding of working memory and its role in learning. Over the next few years, my knowledge grew and I began to seek resources to help me screen and assess students for working memory impairments. I convinced my school teams to get on board and we started to pioneer general education and special education support for students with working memory problems.

Before I begin to share more of my journey, I would like to speak briefly about what I have seen regarding awareness of working memory in education. When I first began, my only knowledge of working memory was how to evaluate it using cognitive measures such as the Woodcock–Johnson III Cognitive or the Wechsler Intelligence Scale for Children (WISC-V). During my graduate studies, I did not receive any training on the role of working memory in learning; neither had many of my colleagues. It has only been through my work as a practitioner that I recognized how valuable working memory is. If school districts do not have school personnel who are equipped to adequately support students with working memory needs, how can these students receive targeted help? This is a particularly important question for school psychologists as they are tasked with helping teachers identify students with learning disabilities and develop classroom interventions.

We know that working memory is closely related to academic learning in basic reading skills, reading comprehension, mathematics calculation, mathematics problem solving, written expression, oral expression, and listening comprehension. These academic skills represent seven of the eight disability areas that fall under the special education category of specific learning disability. When conducting special education evaluations, it is therefore essential for school psychologists to test the working memory skills of students. However, most special education personnel do not assess working memory as part of a learning disabilities referral, nor are they aware of the evidence-based intervention options for treating working memory deficits. Consequently, many students with working memory problems are not identified, and they miss opportunities to learn strategies and receive services that could help them reduce task failure and optimize learning opportunities. These facts led me to develop a program of support to help special education personnel in my district to: (1) understand the role working memory plays in learning; (2) support working memory in the classroom via accommodations and interventions; (3) evaluate working memory impairments using specialized tools; and (4) develop specialized instruction that targets working memory.

Working memory grant

To accomplish these goals I wrote a grant seeking funds from my district's foundation to purchase assessment and intervention tools to support students with working memory impairments. It was one of my proudest moments as a school psychologist when I received word that I was awarded $5000 dollars. Once the elation wore off, I was tasked with leading the development of a district-wide program of support.

My special education department helped me to assemble a committee to research and develop working memory screening, intervention, and assessment procedures. Members of this committee included school psychologists, resource teachers, and speech-language pathologists. It was important that all the specialists who might eventually work with students who qualified for individual education plan (IEP) that targeted working memory and academic concerns participate in the development of the program.

Working memory webinars and presentations

Our working memory committee members and special education personnel received extensive training over a 2-year period from Dr Tracy Alloway and others. This training included webinars and in-person presentations on:

- Working memory theory
- Relationship between working memory and other psychological processes and academic areas
- Screening and assessment of working memory
- Working memory accommodations and interventions

Then our committee delivered a variation of these trainings to elementary school teachers. The feedback has been encouraging:

- *This is new information to me but it is much needed and something I can implement with my students!*
- *I have a student who shows many of the characteristics.*
- *During the presentation I was able to identify a student in my class who might have working memory issues. I had never considered this before and it was very helpful!*
- *I plan to take this information to now observe my students and watch their deficits/characteristics of WM problems. I need to get a handle on*

who I think might be presenting with WM difficulties before I can apply interventions. Anxious to try interventions!

- *I already have several students in mind who could benefit from the interventions discussed.*
- *Great information – will use some of the strategies to help support any students with possible working memory issues.*

Working memory screening

The standardized measures that we use to identify a working memory impairment include the *Working Memory Rating Scale* (WMRS) screener and the *Automated Working Memory Assessment* (AWMA). The latter measure provides us with a comprehensive examination of a student's working memory skills as it provides a measure of both verbal and visual–spatial working memory and short-term memory. Most cognitive measures that provide an index of working memory only measure auditory working memory (e.g., WJ III and WISC-IV); thus, the AWMA is more likely to accurately identify strengths and weaknesses.

Individual education plan (IEP)

Students who have been identified as having a specific learning disability with a weakness in working memory qualify for special education services. Part of the specialized instruction involves cognitive training and strategy instruction. The cognitive training program we utilize is *Jungle Memory*, developed by Dr Ross Alloway. Students work on this program for 15–20 minutes for four or five days a week. After completing the program, a strategy instruction program is implemented. Here is a case study of a student who went through our program.

Case Study: John

John showed evidence of learning problems from an early age. According to the parent report, John first showed signs of learning difficulties in preschool. Throughout elementary school, he attended summer school and received academic tutoring in reading and language.

John was identified for special education services, under the category of speech–language impairment. He received services over a 3-year period targeting language skills. During his triennial IEP review a cognitive assessment was recommended to determine if there were any psychological-processing weaknesses negatively influencing academic learning, as John continued to experience academic challenges in the classroom. Results of the assessment found strengths in some language skills but weaknesses in short-term and working memory, processing speed, and reasoning skills.

Cognitive training: *Jungle Memory*

John showed remarkable progress in all skills targeted by *Jungle Memory*. Following the completion of this program, John's mother and teacher reported the following:

> John has made some great improvements this year. He is completing more of his assignments independently at home and has moved to learning the full spelling list. He seems more motivated to have us sit beside him and help him. (Mother)

> John's math facts have improved. His greatest strength is math, and he is doing a great job this year grasping new skills. He is polite, funny, respectful, with a great work ethic, and he always tries his best. He has shown a lot of progress in his skills this school year. (Classroom teacher)

Working memory accommodations and strategies

Important classroom accommodations that we identified included:

- Provision of written checklists and reminders of step-by-step procedures
- Extended time testing
- Requirement to do no more than one task at a time
- Preferential seating to reduce distractions

When John's case manager asked him some questions about the memory strategies he had learned, he told her that *'None of the memory strategies are hard and they help me to study classroom information better!'* He also reported enthusiastically how he had recently received 100% on a math test. His re-evaluation results showed remarkable improvement from his standardized scores 2 years previously see Table.

(Continued)

(Continued)

John's results: Clinical Evaluation of Language Fundamentals Fourth Edition (CELF-4)

	April 2011		April 2013	
	Standard score	Percentile rank	Standard score	Percentile rank
Core language score	91	27	99	47
Receptive language index	85	16	102	55
Expressive language index	93	32	96	39
Language content index	84	14	96	39
Language memory index	96	39	101	53
Working memory index	72	3	83	17

John showed improvement in all areas assessed. The most dramatic improvements were in his receptive language, language content, and working memory. His receptive language index and his language content scores moved from low average to **average**, and his working memory index scores also increased. Although it is not unheard of to see changes like this, it is unusual.

The case manager attributed the change in his scores to his cognitive training with *Jungle Memory*, strategy instruction, and classroom accommodations. Based on the assessment results and classroom performance data, John was dismissed from special education services. A 504 Plan* was initiated since John continued to need accommodations to help him benefit from instruction. Formal accommodations were written into his plan based on strategies recommended by Dr Tracy Alloway and others. John has responded well to the accommodations and is managing grade-level course work without a need for specialized instruction.

---

* A 504 plan is 'developed by school teams and parents to support the educational needs of a K–12 student with a disability that substantially limits one or more major life activities such as: learning, speaking, listening, reading, writing, concentrating, caring for oneself, and so on' (from the (US)National Center for Learning Disabilities).

In the view of our committee and his former case manager, John is a testament to the success that can be achieved when a student's needs are appropriately identified and targeted with evidence-based assessments and interventions.

Conclusion

The need to develop a school-based program of support for students with working memory problems is both important and timely. We now understand so much more about how the brain functions and how students learn, and it is important to put this knowledge to work. Research has shown that working memory can be improved through cognitive training and strategy instruction. As educators, we should look for the tools and training that will enable us to support students who struggle to remember. Today's students *are* tomorrow's leaders. Let's help them succeed and become all that they can be!

APPENDIX: SUMMARY OF WORKING MEMORY STRATEGIES

Here is a list of the **general working memory strategies** discussed in this book that can be applied to students with general learning needs.

DCD, developmental coordination disorder; ADHD, attention deficit/hyperactivity disorder; ASD, autism spectrum disorder.

	Dyslexia Ch. 3	Dyscalculia Ch. 4	DCD Ch. 5	ADHD Ch. 6	ASD Ch. 7	Anxiety Ch. 8
Use visual representation to support working memory	✓	✓	✓			✓
Shorten activities to reduce the working memory load	✓	✓		✓		✓
Break down information to reduce working memory processing	✓				✓	✓
Reduce working memory processing in activities	✓	✓	✓		✓	
Use learning tools and visual aids to support working memory processing		✓				✓
Model the use of memory aids		✓				
Minimize distractions so working memory is not overwhelmed			✓		✓	✓
Repeat information intermittently to boost working memory				✓		✓

Here is a list of the **specific working memory strategies** discussed in this book targeted for students with a particular disorder.

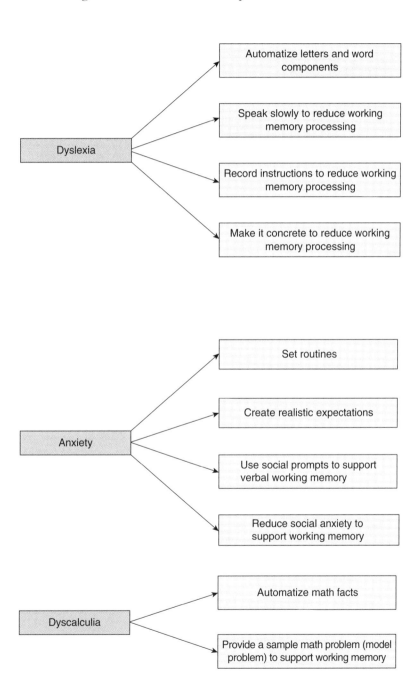

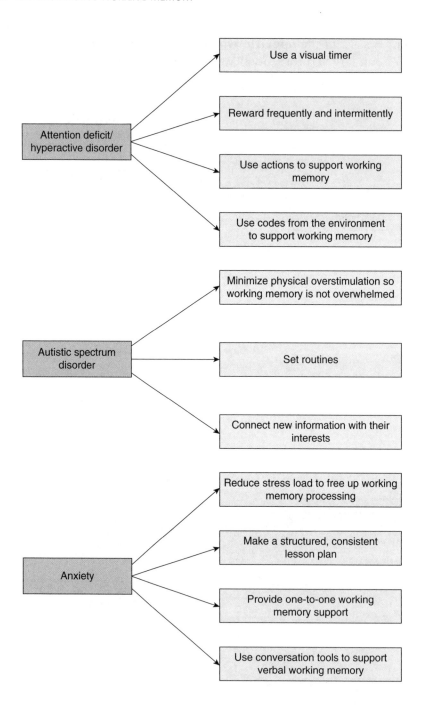

INDEX